The L. Ron Hubbard Series

BRIDGE PUBLICATIONS, INC.
5600 E. Olympic Blvd.
Commerce, California 90022 USA

ISBN 978-1-4031-9892-1

Special acknowledgment is made to the L. Ron Hubbard Library for permission to reproduce photographs from his personal collection. Additional credits: pp. cover, viii, 2, 6, 11, 35, 45, 53, 84 Keystone Press Agency/Hulton Archive; pp. 1, 7, 85, 113, back cover Mushakesa/Shutterstock.com; pp. (background) 22–59, 62–65, 78–81, 92–101, 114 MIXA/Getty Images; pp. (paper) 23, 25–26, 29, 61, 69, 103, 104 Lucy Baldwin/Shutterstock.com; pp. 39–43, 48–52, 55–59, 71, 86, 96, 101 Ken Lauder/Rex Features Ltd.; p. 66 Frescomovie/Shutterstock.com; pp. (paper) 94–95, 99, 114 Myotis/Shutterstock.com.

Articles appearing on pp. 33–34, 37–44, 47–52, 55–59, 65, 79–80 courtesy of *Garden News;* articles appearing on pp. 63, 93 courtesy of *East Grinstead Courier;* p. 99 courtesy of *Toronto Star Archives;* pp. 100–101 courtesy of *Farmers' Weekly,* South Africa.

Printed in the United States of America

The L. Ron Hubbard Series: Horticulture—English

The L. Ron Hubbard Series

HORTICULTURE FOR A GREENER WORLD

Bridge

PUBLICATIONS, INC.®

CONTENTS

Horticulture: For a Greener World

An Introduction to L. Ron Hubbard | 1

Experimental Background | 7

Duties of a Grounds Manager | 12

Grounds Manager *by L. Ron Hubbard* | 13

Experimental Procedure | 22

Grow Lights | 24

The Magic of Seed Irradiation | 32

...In Horticulture | 33

Light and Your Plants | 36

Your Plants ARE Affected by Street Lighting | 37

The Doctor Sheds New Light on Mildew Cure | 38

How Geraniums React to the Light Test | 44

Automating Your Greenhouse | 46

This Automatic Greenhouse Uses Warm Water at Roots | 47

Sowing and Soil | 54

Proof That Peat Moss Is a Failure as a Compost | 55

Pot Test for the Perfect Soil | 56

On Germination Rates | 60

    New Sowing Technique for Improved Germination | 61

The First Crop of 1960 | 62

    First Sweet Corn Crop Raised | 63

Advice and Diagnosis | 64

    Scientist Seeks Your Help in His Research | 65

Methods of Transplanting | 78

    Try This New Way of Transplanting Trees | 79

Advanced Experimentation | 85

The Inner Life of Plants Revealed | 88

    Summary of Advanced Experimentation *by L. Ron Hubbard* | 89

Revolution Rocks the Plant Kingdom! | 92

    Can Plants Think? He Asks | 93

    Can Plants Think? Yes, Says a Nuclear Physicist! | 97

    Plants Can Worry and Feel Pain | 100

An Insider's View | 102

    Mr. Hubbard's Horticultural Research | 103

Corollary Discoveries | 106

Change & Recovery *by L. Ron Hubbard* | 107

Cultural Outgrowth | 113

Closing Note | 117

Appendix

Glossary | 121

Index | 151

An Introduction to
L. Ron Hubbard

*I*N THE SPRING OF 1959 AND THE WAKE OF EXPERIMENTATION within L. Ron Hubbard's greenhouse laboratory at Saint Hill Manor in East Grinstead, Sussex, the world of British horticulture quite factually announced: "A discovery of immense significance to all gardeners has been made." By the winter of 1960, and with BBC interviews of L. Ron Hubbard airing to millions, it was mainstream: "Revolution rocks the plant kingdom!" declared the Sunday supplements, and "Never in all the eons have plants created such a stir." Then came the derivative studies of what a scientific community hailed as "an infallible test of the presence of life," while global headlines continued proclaiming: "Plants have feelings, too." Whereupon, a whole new cultural mind-set took root and everyone was suddenly speaking of what L. Ron Hubbard described as an *interwoven partnership for the survival of everything that is alive.*

Welcome to a very special issue of the *L. Ron Hubbard Series.* Through the pages to follow, we shall track the full course of Ron's horticultural discoveries from the particulars of planting, seeding, fertilization and harvesting toward a newfound vision of all living things.

We shall further consider what he discovered as regards the elemental force behind all cultivation and what it revealed as regards the essence of life itself—very much including human beings. Finally, we shall consider all else bearing fruit in L. Ron Hubbard's greenhouse, including crops of such prodigious size and yield that reporters could not help but envision a day when global food resources increase to such abundance no human being need ever suffer starvation again.

By way of introduction, however, let us dispel a few minor misconceptions. In the first place, while the horticulturists of 1959 regarded L. Ron Hubbard's work as a bolt from the blue, in fact he had long examined questions pertaining to life sources and life energies. Indeed, the entire thrust of his greater life's journey as realized with the

The newly ensconced master of Saint Hill Manor,
East Grinstead, Sussex, 1959

Scientology religion followed from just such an examination—specifically, his isolation of the human spirit as the *Source of all*. In that regard, what transpired in L. Ron Hubbard's Saint Hill greenhouse actually comprised but a correlative study to his greater contribution. That is, and very simply: here was the first scientific effort to ascertain if what we call vegetable life is actually the same *order of life* as that which exists in Man. (It is, and dramatically so, but we get ahead of our story.) More to our immediate point: in bringing fundamental truths of Scientology to his horticultural laboratory in southern England, L. Ron Hubbard not only revolutionized the world of horticulture, he revolutionized world thinking.

Needless to say, then, this story extends well beyond that famed Saint Hill greenhouse and factually includes much of what drives today's environmental movements. It was L. Ron Hubbard, for example, who provided a good deal of what comprises the philosophic basis of environmental consciousness, including what he described as our *cooperation* with all other living things. Then again, he was among the first to install a fully automated greenhouse for English flower and vegetable cultivation, the first again to successfully mutate English seeds with low-energy, or "soft," radiation and likewise the first to codify frequencies of artificial grow lights according to plant type and rate of growth. And if only to cite but one word of results: previously skeptical reporters were soon astounded at what they described as the veritable "food of the gods."

So let us proceed into a wondrous world of mysteries unveiled amidst verdant flower beds and rows of prodigious cornstalks. Needless to say, it is a tale best told by those who actually witnessed it—very much including astonished English gardeners and amazed British journalists. But also needless to say, it is a story of transcendent revelations and global repercussions, which is why we best begin with L. Ron Hubbard's own preliminary word on horticulture: *"It is a large subject."* ■

Inspecting an orchid come back to life with
Saint Hill Grounds Manager Herbert D. Hall

CHAPTER ONE

Experimental BACKGROUND

Experimental
Background

WITH THE METEORIC GROWTH OF SCIENTOLOGY through the latter 1950s, L. Ron Hubbard embarked upon a search for an international training and administrative headquarters that would accommodate all Scientology functions. In particular, he wished for a center conveniently accessible to

Scientologists from both the United States and British Commonwealth and yet still providing a measure of tranquility for his continuing research on behalf of Scientology. That center became Saint Hill Manor, East Grinstead, Sussex. The estate itself boasted a considerable history and masters were quite naturally the focus of local attention. (The previous owner to L. Ron Hubbard, for example, was a highly colorful Maharajah of Jaipur.) Thus, quite apart from L. Ron Hubbard's worldwide renown as the Founder of Dianetics and Scientology, his occupancy at Saint Hill sparked keen local interest. Moreover, his announcement of forthcoming horticultural experimentation to inquiring journalists from the *East Grinstead Courier* particularly intrigued residents of a region where pastoral traditions ran very deep indeed.

As a general word of background to that first round of experimentation, Ron returns us to January 1916 and a propitious journey from his boyhood home in Helena, Montana, to the California coast. There, and albeit barely five years old, he tells how the cultivation of off-season produce sparked an early interest in horticultural fundamentals. Most especially: "It would fascinate me to know that the sun would be shining, and fruits and vegetables growing, while other parts of the world were in the grip of winter." Hence, his subsequent study of winter cultivation and particularly hothouse production. Hence, too, his later greenhouse designs for flower cultivation in notoriously inhospitable winters of the American Northwest. And hence, his first experimental goal of 1959: *"To improve and diversify world food production."*

Above
L. Ron Hubbard's
Horticultural
Research Station,
1959

Right
An appropriately
foliated path to a
then renowned
Saint Hill
glasshouse

Additionally by way of background to what would soon germinate at Saint Hill, Ron returns us to a prerevolutionary China circa 1928. Those familiar with the developmental history of Dianetics and Scientology will recall it as the landscape of his early inquiries into a spiritual dimension and where he first encountered phenomena well beyond bounds of Western science. By the same token, however, China was also the land where he first encountered an aching material need and cyclical famine exacerbated by a lack of agricultural know-how. In eventual reply came his papers from a Naval School of Military Government at Princeton University where, preparatory to service with United States occupation forces, he expressly called for a reformation of agricultural methods. In particular: the development of local fertilizers, the importation of nutritionally rich soya beans and scientifically rotated crops.

That he attended the first United States class on atomic and molecular theory while a sophomore at George Washington University provides still another angle on what follows here. That is, and particularly given a 1957 series of lectures on radioactive fallout inspiring debate within the British Parliament, it was only natural journalists addressed the man as "Dr. Hubbard" and described him as a nuclear physicist.

As we shall see, and in accord with all the above, he would approach this science of horticulture from every conceivable angle: disease control through soft radiation bombardment, temperature regulation, fertilization, irrigation, soil management and lighting. As noted, he was also among the first to generate mutant seeds for increased crop yield—most immediately, tomato seeds.

As for what else may be said in an anticipation of articles to follow from the spring of 1959, one

Above
Yet another view of Dr. Hubbard's Research Station amidst the sylvan glades of Sussex woodlands

should bear in mind that all experimentation was conducted in parallel fashion. Thus while chapters are arranged sequentially by subject, all must be viewed as occurring simultaneously. Moreover, all stood quite in advance of traditional practice. Thus, for example, the Saint Hill Manor greenhouse was originally nothing of what one finds reported in articles to follow. Indeed, the Maharajah employed the facility solely for his peaches and geraniums. Similarly, even members of England's Atomic Gardening Society—or those most dedicated to the possibilities of seed radiation—had never previously glimpsed the X-ray equipment L. Ron Hubbard housed in the Maharajah's wine cellar.

Finally, let us also bear in mind what so many journalists did not. While British horticulture is both ancient and honorable, and there is nothing so wonderfully natural as an English garden, the craft is actually closer to art than science. Thus, while infrared mildew control and light spectrum analysis were generally known subjects, no one had sifted garden soil with quite the same eye as the Founder of Scientology. Then, too, no one had examined plant life in terms of sentient response and what, in fact, amounted to *emotions*. In short, then, L. Ron Hubbard was about to address problems of plant growth and care with the same exacting methodology with which he isolated the fundamental truths of Scientology. Moreover, he was about to do so from the same far-reaching viewpoint and to the same universal end—*prosperity for all.* ◾

The LRH Office at Saint Hill Manor with a text entitled
Gardens & Grounds That Take Care of Themselves
by home and gardens maven Amelia Leavitt Hill

Duties of a Grounds Manager

It has been said there is nothing quite so harmonious with nature as the free-form English gardening tradition. Meandering paths, irregular beds, a profusion of woodland flowers—such are the charms of a minimally pruned and moderately weeded British garden. Yet precisely what lends charm to the free-form garden tends to defeat the market gardener: parasitic mildew, inadequate lighting, inconsistent watering and improper bedding—all these and more were too typically left to chance. Thus comes what agriculturalists would soon describe as Dr. Hubbard's "agrotechnical" methods and a codified regimen of greenhouse maintenance.

It was initially expressed as an instructional memo to Grounds Manager Herbert D. Hall and authored through the first days of summer 1959. Although Mr. Hall had long occupied a Gardener's Cottage along the rim of Saint Hill downs, automated greenhouse production represented entirely new terrain. Thus, in essence, Ron is providing the man with an Estates Manager job description. That he further provides a word on apocryphal green thumbs, or those with exceptional horticultural talents, is actually far more significant than even Mr. Hall might have presumed; for here was the realm into which they were headed and—as we shall see—the horizon was unlimited. ∎

GROUNDS MANAGER

by L. RON HUBBARD

Watering

It will be found that watering requires an exact routine and would absorb a considerable amount of time unless it is carefully planned.

Regular soakings, rather than superficial spraying, will be found to be much more satisfactory.

When watering is superficially done, it will be found that the roots of the plants turn up towards the surface of the ground and they will not be able to obtain proper moisture and will kill easily.

All basic Greenhouse and garden watering is done by sprayer or by watering can, not by hand-held hose. The pressure is seldom adequate, but more importantly, no adequate wetting of the ground can be done by hose.

In dry weather no hour of the day should pass without a sprinkler going somewhere. The sprinkler is turned on over the usual small area that it covers and is left until the ground is thoroughly soaked to a good depth. While this is happening, other work can be done. One comes back and, in passing, changes the position of the sprinkler to a new area.

Watering in Glasshouses

It is not the amount of water on a plant which accelerates its growth. It is the humidity in the air. This humidity must be maintained in a Glasshouse to an adequate temperature. If it is, then high levels of heat, which are desired in a Glasshouse, can be utilized. These levels of heat cannot be utilized if the air in the house is dry, since plants will wither. Therefore all Glasshouse watering is planned on the basis of keeping the air humid, not just keeping the plants watered. Therefore sprinklers are far more use in Glasshouses than watering cans.

LRH and H. D. Hall as glimpsed from atop the Manor

The ordinary procedure of watering in a Glasshouse is to turn on a sprinkler for an adequate length of time to thoroughly soak the ground, the beds or boxes. The sprinkler is aimed preferably at earth rather than boxes and any earth available in the house is thoroughly and deeply soaked regularly.

One does not wait until the earth of a Glasshouse turns gray to resprinkle the house. The earth in a Glasshouse should at all times be black with water.

Before, during or after a thorough wetting of a Glasshouse with a sprinkler, one takes a watering can, in the case of beds, and, removing the spray nozzle, scoops water copiously from the well in the house and lavishes it upon any bed, box or ground area which is not ordinarily reached by a sprinkler system. Such ground beds or boxes are kept soaked and must at all times be wet. They must not be permitted to get so dry as to appear gray.

The test of adequate watering in a Glasshouse is grayness of soil. There must be no gray soil in a Glasshouse if the Glasshouse is properly watered. This is true of a Potting House, seed boxes or a Vine House.

Purpose of Glasshouses

The purpose of a Glasshouse is to permit growing at extremely high-range temperatures in thickly humidified air, otherwise there is no point in using a Glasshouse. Glasshouses are not used just to protect from weather or to stabilize temperature or just to grow things in. They are highly specialized areas which utilize the fact that plants grow quickly in high temperatures if the air is thoroughly humidified.

To keep a Glasshouse at 70 degrees is not to use one at all. Unless the daytime temperature of a Glasshouse can be kept around 95 degrees, with the humidity close to 100% of saturation, one might as well do his gardening outside. A Glasshouse permits high-pressure gardening. It is therefore tightly packed, heavily fertilized, highly humidified and kept very, very hot.

Dangers of a Glasshouse

A Glasshouse is dangerous to use if one neglects watering. Failure to water a Glasshouse can cause a chill of all of its plants in 48 hours.

If the temperature were to go to 125 degrees in a Glasshouse without adequate humidity, everything in it would wither, and if this condition continued for two consecutive days, there would be no crop.

A Glasshouse is something like a rifle. It is very handy to use, but it has two ends.

If a Glasshouse is to get no watering or attention for a 24-hour period, *all* doors and vents should be open full during the summertime. This does not permit the Glasshouse to be functional and accelerate the growth of plants, but neither does it kill plants.

The opening of ports or doors of a Glasshouse for anything but getting across a period when the place will not be watered is a waste of a Glasshouse.

Above left
Glasshouse
sprinkler system
to maintain
a consistent
100 percent
humidity

Below left
Close-up of
thermostat
to regulate
temperatures
at a peak
100 degrees

Glasshouse Temperature

The temperature in a Glasshouse should not be below 60 degrees for more than 3 or 4 hours out of the 24. This is accomplished by closing the Glasshouse thoroughly about five o'clock in the evening or perhaps a little sooner. Upper operating temperature of the Glasshouses are far above what the ordinary amateur gardener supposes. Bedding plants and tomatoes do extremely well at 110 degrees. During the daylight hours, the Glasshouse should not fall much below this.

It requires a certain amount of nerve and a great deal of watchfulness to run a Glasshouse at high temperature, but unless it is run at high temperatures, it is not fulfilling its purpose and the crop might as well be planted outside.

Bedding Plants

Almost all germinations occur best at the highest-level temperatures. In fact, germination is usually assisted when one does not have a Glasshouse, by placing seed boxes in a stove if one is in a hurry.

Watering at least twice daily is required when raising boxes full of bedding plants from seed. This is usually done from a can so that it can be regulated, some species requiring more water than others.

A high level of humidity is required in a house where bedding plants are being started.

Even the boxes of the bedding plants should be wetted. Particularly when pressed peat-moss pots are used, it is necessary to give good attention to watering, since the peat moss absorbs the water away from the plant more rapidly, providing drying occurs.

Cold Frames

Cold frames are not watered, they are flooded. One takes an ordinary hose and puts it in the corner of a cold frame and tries to achieve a saturation of water which will leave actual water on the surface of the soil.

By using a mulch (one that will not exude gas), it will be found that less frequent water is necessary in a cold frame, particularly for melons and similar produce.

After having flooded a cold frame, it is routinely watched and checked to make sure that the humidity and moisture level is adequate. As soon as the ground in the frame begins to gray, flooding is repeated. This may not have to be done oftener than once a week if the mulch is adequate and the weather is not excessively hot. However, it must be checked daily.

In flooding a cold frame, the same principle as that used in sprinkling is applied. One turns on the hose and goes away about other work and comes back to check on it or, when it is flooded, puts the hose in the next frame or, when all frames are done, turns the water off.

Cucumber Shed

A Glasshouse which houses melons and cucumbers must never be permitted to acquire gray earth. Further, it must never be permitted to have low daytime temperatures except when it is actually necessary to air the house, as in the case of gaseous mulches. The Cucumber Shed is run at the highest possible temperatures.

Cucumbers love high temperatures, so do melons. These grow best on earth where ground temperatures in the daytime are routinely in advance of 100 degrees. A house temperature of 125 degrees will not harm cucumbers or melons, *providing* the humidity is adequate.

A Cucumber Shed run at this high-level temperature will produce cucumbers and melons rapidly and in profusion. As in the case of all other Glasshouse work, one's expectancy of yield and rapidity of growth based on planting exterior to Glasshouse and cold frames should not deter one from running a Cucumber Shed for fast growth and fast yield. Cucumbers and melons will grow to maturity with the right handling under glass in one-third the time required in outside planting, providing one handles his heat and water cleverly.

As in the case of any cold frame or Glasshouse, a Cucumber Shed should be thoroughly closed up in the late afternoon, thus retaining the day's heat.

Great care should be taken not to have any air leaks in a Cucumber Shed, so that the warmth will carry forward until well after midnight. This gives at least 16 hours of high temperature in the summertime, with a slack in temperature occurring between 2 A.M. and 8 A.M.

The lowest temperatures on cucumbers should never be less than 50 degrees. There is no actual limit for high temperatures in this particular species, providing humidity is adequate.

Summary

The handling of Glasshouses is usually done timidly or inadequately and the worth and value of a Glasshouse is largely lost among many operators. They prefer to use little water and cut temperatures down to temperatures they can stand. This is only humanly natural. A human being does not live well with the temperature at 122 degrees and the humidity at 100%.

Human beings, however, are not plants. Plants do best in 100% saturation of humidity and, except special cuttings (which are not plants, but which are attempts to make plants from bits of other plants, an entirely different operation than bedding plants and raising crops), temperatures in excess of 100 degrees.

There is a natural timidity on the part of a man to make plants experience things he himself cannot experience. Therefore it is natural for someone to flinch, to open the air vents, to cut down the water supply, to make living conditions that he himself can more easily experience. However, he is making a grave mistake if he does this. He is extending the growth period of the crops in the house as much as three times, because the temperatures will rise and, by reducing the amount of moisture, he is actually risking the entire crop.

The essence of Glasshouse work is fast, hard driving. Don't spare the water, don't spare the fuel or heat. Turn the sprinklers on and leave the vents closed and, in most vine crops and indeed most flower and vegetable crops, it will be found that one wins every time.

Cut down any ideas of any excessive heat in the house by using a sprinkler, not by opening the vents.

Flowers, vegetables, vines grow much faster and more furiously in those parts of the world where the temperature is NORMAL at 110 degrees F and 100% saturation of humidity. If you don't believe it, try to walk through a jungle. This, in essence, is what you are trying to create in a Glasshouse—a jungle. In a jungle, ordinary Northern Hemisphere variety of string beans grow to 2½ feet in length. Melons grow to a foot and a half in diameter, which in the Northern Hemisphere would be considered large at 8 inches in diameter.

The only reason flavor of these productions is in any way impaired lies in the field of plant feeding.

Plant Feeding

If you are going to drive plants fast, you must catalyze their ability to draw sustenance from the soil. Therefore no method of fertilizing, as used in an open field, is satisfactory or applicable in a Glasshouse. In a jungle, plants which grow too rapidly are growing usually on very badly starved ground. This ground has been grown on so often and is in such a state of gaseousness and decay that it is a wonder that the plants and their fruit have any flavor at all.

If you are going to drive plants as hard as they are driven in a jungle, you have to feed them as hard.

No 2 weeks must be permitted to go by in a Glasshouse where actual growing is taking place without an application of food to the soil.

This is not done by a spray. It is done by means of crystalline form applied to the plants in such a way as not to rest upon the leaves. In view of the fact that heavy watering is taking place routinely, a great deal of this plant food is carried away or carried too deeply into the soil to be available to the plants.

Right "This, in essence, is what you are trying to create in a Glasshouse—a jungle" —LRH

Above
Mr. Hall
examines
the fruition
of tungsten
lighting

It takes approximately 10 days for commercial nitrates and phosphates to be in any way effective. Therefore it will not be until 10 days after the summer monthly feeding that the food is effective. Thus the Glasshouse is prepared in advance, or the box is prepared in advance, by a period of as much as 10 days.

Every 2 weeks thereafter, a good quantity of commercial fertilizer is applied.

It is sometimes also necessary to apply minerals to the soil. The application of minerals is totally dependent upon the particular minerals used by particular plants. Usually any soil has enough minerals in it to last the plant quite a while, but the artificial implanting of minerals in the soil is necessary if one wishes to maintain the flavor of a crop.

In the presence of a great deal of watering, a great deal of fertilizing is necessary. If things are to grow with three times the speed, they must be fed with three times the food.

Watering, then, gives us the additional problem of additional fertilizing.

If one really means to grow a crop in a Glasshouse and if one is not trying to not grow a crop, then the only choice he has is to feed heavily, water heavily and keep the heat up.

The result of such a program is heavy, good, flavorable, disease-free food.

Spraying

It is a maxim that healthy plants do not need a great deal of spraying. If they are kept free from weeds, are well fertilized, well watered and given high heat, their enthusiasm overcomes ordinary diseases. In fact, the heat itself is usually above the level of most diseases to tolerate. This is also true of worms.

If spraying is undertaken, it must be remembered that a great deal of watering by sprinklers is also undertaken. The excess spray washes off into the soil and tends to some degree to retard the growth of the plants. Therefore spraying is done in small doses and is done only when and where it is needed.

It is better to amputate a disease out of a Greenhouse than to try to spray it out.

The Green Thumb

We have, all of us, heard the superstition of the green thumb.

It actually has a very simple explanation. A person with a green thumb has a DESIRE TO MAKE PLANTS GROW.

The people who do not have a green thumb will be found to be detectable outside the bounds of superstition. There is no superstition about it. Some parts of their nature restrains them from giving adequate attention to plants. This will be found in small ways having to do with forgetting or accidents or minor omissions in plant care.

Just as you will find some mothers cutting down on the amount of oatmeal little Johnny will have, when as a matter of fact no quantity of oatmeal would ever hurt Johnny, so you will find some gardeners cutting down on water, cutting down on fertilizer and cutting down on heat. Unknown to them, some part of their nature is causing them to restrain plants from growing.

Plants require a lot of enthusiasm. They almost need a cheering section, but in addition to this, they need water, heat, care and, above that, good planning.

A person with a green thumb simply is not restraining plants from growing. A green thumb is not a positive application of any one thing. It is the absence of denial. A person who denies plants does not have a green thumb.

All you have to do is to want plants to grow and have no qualms about them growing, and take the time necessary to give them food and water after applying a reasonable amount of good sense to planning it out and you have a green thumb.

In hiring personnel to work about Greenhouses, keep a sharp eye out for the man who forgets watering or who makes small mistakes. Plants will not prosper around him. He has something in his nature which tries to forbid plants to grow. He does not really want to have them grow—thus he forgets things and makes small omissions. Frankly, in operating any wide venture having to do with plants, such a person is a considerable liability. He must be weeded out of any crew before he can do real damage.

Oddly enough, it will be found that the man who will let plants grow has a fairly sunny disposition, is not upset and crabby at everything in sight and gets along fairly well with other people. Thus we accomplish a rule in hiring that we want men who get along with other people and who do not make mistakes with plants. Thus we will all prosper.

Experimental Procedure

Notwithstanding the inherent charm of an English garden bending to the whims of Mother Nature, the beauty is frequently fleeting. Witness the especially persistent strains of mold and mildew attacking leaves through cloud-capped winters. Witness, too, the risks of uncontrolled lighting, inconsistent planting and variable soil chemistry on fragile shoots. In short, witness the exacting detail with which L. Ron Hubbard dissected every facet bearing on the horticultural process and then devised an experimental procedure to determine what would best flourish.

What then follows through succeeding pages is exactly that: the experimental procedure and subsequent coverage in gardening periodicals. That all experimentation was conducted through what amounted to the same fruitful season underscores the fact he was about to examine the entirety of plant life. Which is to say: both physical response to environmental factors and what qualifies as the emotional response. That experimental protocol was strictly observed and even seemingly minute changes in plant vitality were faithfully recorded further underscores why British gardeners dubbed Dr. Hubbard's Saint Hill greenhouse, the Sussex Research Station.

Finally, and above all, let us bear in mind that here is agriculture for the populace at large. That is to say, here is not an ornamental garden of trellised walls, leafy grottoes and waterlilies. Rather, here are table vegetables, cattle feed and sweet corn. Here, too, is a study of all factors relative to market garden growth, including: spectrum analysis, infrared mildew control, soil content and sowing techniques. While if only to cap it: here is also that deeper link between plant life and the rest of life...and thus a cornucopia of life. ■

June 26th 1959

EXPERIMENTAL PROJECT 1

To test fodder potential of Golden Hummer corn and Golden Cross Bantam (Hybrid) for cattle feeding. Two rows of each were sown in upper one acre on June 2nd. Rows three feet apart and kernels placed in hills one foot apart, covered with one inch of soil.

Soil conditions

These seeds were sown under dry hard abnormal field conditions, the soil being cultivated only enough to permit drills to be made to allow the seeds to be covered.

Weather

At the time of sowing there had only been one day of light rain in the previous two weeks, and at no time had any measurable amount of rain fallen to assist in the germination of the seeds after sowing. The temperature around 60 to 65 degrees was about average air temperature, for an exposed field in June.

Germination

It was found that the germination of the Golden Hummer corn was slightly better than the Golden Bantam Hybrid. This of course could possibly be due to the large quantities of turf fibre and weed accumulation in different parts of the plot used for the experiment which attracted the attention of birds.

On the whole germination was about 75%, and shoots from both corns appeared within *nine days* giving us a plant that will flourish under neglected conditions.

Grow Lights

Original project notes from Ron's benchmark test of the grow-light spectrum. Among the most fruitful and illuminating experiments conducted at the Saint Hill Research Station, here was a first definitive examination of light quality and wavelength on a classic English garden; while in consequence came what amounted to a perpetual growing season. ■

Saint Hill Estates
East Grinstead
Sussex

Experimental Project 3

Purpose: To determine the most favorable conditions of growth using lamps of various character to assist sunlight for various commercial items and to obtain time of growth and flowering or fruiting.

Equipment: A Bench Glasshouse (Pothouse) and numerous lamps and devices.

The planting of the center table of pothouse will be as follows:
In *each* set of 15 10-inch pots we will test the following:

Class I – 2 vine plants
Class II – 4 root plants
Class III – 2 potted flower plants
Class IV – 2 trees
Class V – 2 shrubs
Class VI – 2 bush vegetables
Class VII – 2 flowering bushes
Class VIII – 2 stalk plants

These we will give class numbers as noted so we can keep notes in brief.

The varieties will be as follows by *pots*. (More than one plant *can* go in in pot but some can have only one plant.)

Each class is represented in each group:

Class I

Pot 1 – English Tomato (3 plants)
Pot 2 – Red Cherry Tomato (3 plants)

Class II

Pot 3 – Radishes and Beets
Pot 4 – Turnips and Potatoes

Class III

Pot 5 – Geraniums
Pot 6 – Chrysanthemums

Class IV

Pot 7 – Scotch Fir 6 to 12 inches high but all of same height
Pot 8 – Native Willow 6 to 12 inches high but all of same height

Class V

Pot 9 – Rhodie (already rooted) & 2 cuttings, 1 cut, 1 broken
Pot 10 – Azalea (already rooted)

Class VI

Pot 11 – Dwarf Pea
Pot 12 – Dwarf Bean

Class VII

Pot 13 – Rose plant & 3 Rose cuttings
Pot 14 – Hydrangea & 3 Hydrangea cuttings

Class VIII

Pot 15 – American Sweet Corn Golden Hummer and South American Popcorn

These are planted as a group in 15 10-inch pots and is the typical group to be tested. There will be 4 of these groups in the large section of the pothouse and 1 of these groups in the middle of the table in the smaller division. Also, 1 of these groups will be placed outside where it will get average sun and weather but no special lighting.

These groups will be numbered by painted signs hung on table before them and below as per example.

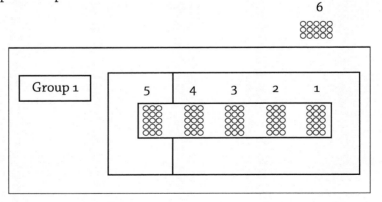

The arrangement of each group will be the same in each case. They are numbered from left to right beginning nearest the pothouse door.

Box Test

One pot of plants (10 inch)
and one light will be   near
placed in each box.
The plants should be   t up
as follows:
    2 tomatoes, small plants
    2 radishes   be
    2 lettuces   al
They are placed as follows: planted
The two tomatoes at one side,   and
The lettuces in the center and   from
seed in the pot. already grown above surface
    One such pot is put in   owing
each box and we then   lities
    of growth already remedied
and equalized before we go
into light test stage.

The labels in the pots bear no names, only the group, class and pot number. This speeds recording.

1–IV–8 is a typical designation meaning Group 1 (Arabic Numeral) Class IV (Roman Numeral) Pot 8 (Arabic Numeral). In decoding records we find this was Group 1 (given artificial sunlight at night) Class IV (trees) Pot 8 (Native Willow).

Without a recording system the writing of notes becomes staggering. And for that matter, without such order, experiments become worthless or tell lies.

Our procedure in reading and recording will be to measure height of plant with a special rule giving two perpendiculars, and width of largest leaf with same rule.

Condition will also be recorded by code—namely A for Excellent, B for ok, C for Poor, D for Awful. This is based on leaf condition seen by daylight.

Thus we record off only ninety-five observations a day and can note these in an hour and a half, taking it easy. We start recording always at 3:30 PM.

The remaining spaces in the pothouse center table will be filled with large 10-inch pots of earth and totally planted in English leaf lettuce to grow in place, not transplant. The side tables will be planted in marketable boxes of plants and, where we have pots, with geraniums from our cuttings. We will market all this extra in due course. We need it to provide a proper humidity. As we market we will replace.

The light types we will use on groups are as follows:

> Group 1 – Artificial Daylight Siemens Type MAT/V Clear bulb and reflector
> 300 Watts
>
> Group 2 – Ordinary tungsten lamp light, 300 W Clear bulb and reflector
>
> Group 3 – Infra-red Clear bulbs, 250 W Siemens and reflector
>
> Group 4 – 2 ultra-violet type MBW/U 125 W Siemens
>
> Group 5 – No light from lamp
>
> Group 6 – Outside, no light from any lamps

Duration of Test

We will continue test on a recording basis until first group to do so bears fruit. We will continue lights until the leading groups produce. Then we will compare quality and flavor of products.

Thereafter we will fit house with most favorable result equipment and produce a test commercial crop of the most desirable plants or fruit.

We will plant trees from experiment at most needed replacement spots on estate.

Dr. Hubbard

Weather Cloudy - Warm
Athose Temp - 84 - 66 in last 24 hrs.

1 - I - 1 (Diseased plant removed leaving 2 plants)		all		
	Healthy - A	11" - 1¼		
1 - I - 2	Healthy B	5 5/16 - 1 2/16 Rad		
1 - II - 3	" B	2 6/16 - 1¼ Pot		
1 - II - 4	" A	2 4/16 - 1¼		
1 - III - 5	" B	7 3/4 - 2 3/4		
1 - III - 6	" C	15 - 4 3/4		
1 - IV - 7 Healthy	C	4 3/4 - 4/32		
1 - IV - 8 Awful	C	10½ - 3/4		
1 - V - 9 Fair Healthy	A&C 5¼ - 1 6/86			
1 - V - 10 Poor	A&C 11 - 3/4			
1 - VI - 11 Good	A	1 - 7/86		
1 - VI - 12 Good -	A	4 - 2½		
1 - VII - 13 Fair -	A	12½ - 3/4		
1 - VII - 14 Poor -	C	12 - 3 5/86		
1 - VIII - 15 Good	B	5 - 3/4		
2 - 1 - 1 Good	A	12½ 1 5/16		
2 - 1 - 2 Fair	B+	4 14/16 3/4		
2 - 11 - 3 Healthy	B	2 13/16 1 3/16 Pot.		
2 - 11 - 4 Healthy	A	1½ 1/16		
2 - 111 - 5 Healthy	B	9" 2 19/16		
2 - 111 - 6 Fair	B	12" 3 3/4		
2 - IV - 7 Fair	B.	7 7/16 1/32		
2 - IV - 8 DEAD	D	1" 4/8 curled		
2 - V - 9 Fair	C	5 4/16 1 19/16		
2 - V - 10 Healthy	A	13 6/16 13/16		
2 - VI - 11 Healthy	A	1" 7/16		
2 - VI - 12 Healthy	A	3 9/16 2½		
2 - VII - 13 Poor.	A	10 7/16 1 10/16		
2 - VII - 14 Fair	C	12½ 3 1/16		
2 - VIII - 15 Healthy	B	4 12/16 19/16		
3 - I - 1 Diseased	A	10¼ - 2		
3 - I - 2 1 plant removed, Black Stripe - 5 3/4	15/16			
3 - II - 3 healthy	A	2 3/4 15/16		
3 - II - 4 "	A	2½ 15/16 Potatox		
3 - III - 5 Blight (Fair) A	8½ 2¼			
3 - III - 6 Poor	B	14¼ 4		
3 - IV - 7 healthy	A	7 1/32		
3 - IV - 8 - Dead	D	12 14/16 curled		
3 - V - 9 - Poor	C	5 2/16 1 3/4		
3 - V - 10 - Good	A	11 10/16 1"		

July 13, 1959

Experimental Project 5

Consisting of 6 groups of plants
served under various conditions:

Group 1 — Artificial Sunlight + hthse light
Group 2 — Tungsten   + "   "
Group 3 — Infra Red   + "   "
Group 4 — Ultra Violet   + "   "
Group 5 — Usual hothouse sunlight + "   "
Group 6 — Outdoors, no artificial heat or light

Experiment 4:45 PM Monday July 13, 1959
Recorded at St Hill about 3 & 5 PM daily.

Experimental ledger book bearing
L. Ron Hubbard's handwritten
notations on plant growth
relative to light source,
greenhouse temperature
and weather

The Magic of Seed Irradiation

Although Britain's Atomic Garden Club had enthusiastically irradiated seeds for years, nothing compared to the resilient new strains of vegetables and wildflowers emerging from a Saint Hill X-ray laboratory. Indeed, visitors would liken it to an alchemical process whereby a hundred years of horticultural breeding was effected in a matter of hours. The secret lay with that gentle bombardment of soft radiation to rearrange the genetic "blueprint" of seeds. The result was a veritable explosion of tomatoes on the truss and all as dutifully reported in a first Garden News feature on Dr. Hubbard's horticultural miracles. ∎

...IN HORTICULTURE

A REVOLUTION IS FORECAST BY AMERICAN Nuclear Scientist, Dr. Lafayette Hubbard, a leading authority on plant life, whose experiments concern the effects of radio-activity on seeds and plants. And Dr. Hubbard is preparing to incorporate his equipment and ultra-modern greenhouse at his newly-acquired Sussex estate of Saint Hill Manor near East Grinstead.

Dr. Hubbard quite freely prophesies that in only a few years time his work will lead to a world-wide revolution in the world of horticulture.

Already his knowledge and experiments have taken him into the depths of the unknown in horticulture. By special processes he has:

Developed incredible strains of plants and...

Discovered ways of controlling the growth and development of plants to such an extent that he is able to increase their productivity of flowers or fruits many times.

And all this is done through the medium of radio-active waves, using infra-red, ultra-violet, or X-ray according to requirements.

Dr. Hubbard explained his experiments: "A seed is like a blueprint, X-rays and gamma rays

Five times the yield per plant

re-arrange this blueprint so that you have a highly developed strain of, say, chrysanthemum, then by battering seeds from this flower and rearing them in the normal way the original strain can be produced. On the other hand, it is also possible to produce an even better strain than the one started with.

"If the particular seeds receive too large a dose of the rays they go back to their original strain, but if they have too small an amount the results are freak plants, with perhaps no leaves or purple flowers—it can be quite amazing," he said.

Dr. Hubbard told me that the advantages of such treatment are obvious: it would mean that commercial growers could offer cucumber seeds that would give five times the number of cucumbers and tomato plants that could produce five times the number of tomatoes which might be expected from present strains.

But vines are Dr. Hubbard's pet interest.... "I like them because they don't mind being pushed around. With my treatment they react in the most amazing ways," he joked.

At present he is pursuing his maxim—"look, don't think"—by segregating a group of vines which have been treated with radio-active waves and those that have not. He planted them at the same time, and under the same conditions. And the treated plants are well in advance of the others after only a few weeks in the greenhouse.

Another line of research which he is conducting enables plants to grow by day—and night. For the commercial gardener this cuts growing time more than half, with the resulting increase in saleable stock.

And so, as Dr. Hubbard continues with his experiments in the peaceful surroundings of his Sussex estate (he says that he has no need or interest in commercialising his findings) the horticultural world awaits results which will ultimately benefit both amateur and professional gardeners.

Light and Your Plants

In a perfect horticultural environment, artificial plant light stimulates growth with an electromagnetic spectrum appropriate for photosynthesis. Thus the "grow light" typically mimics natural light to which a particular plant is best adapted. But, oh, the inconsistencies and variables! And, oh, how heated the contention between sodium versus fluorescent or mercury vapor versus clear tungsten bulbs.

In what was then rightly regarded as an expedient reply comes the Garden News spotlight on the Dr. Hubbard's "infrared mildew cure" and his larger analysis of light spectrum and growth rate. Irrespective of traditional belief in red/blue grow lights, Ron's benchmark experimentation determined yellow light to be most beneficial for plant growth. Hence, the original double-page spread and subsequent follow-up article. ■

YOUR PLANTS ARE AFFECTED BY STREET LIGHTING

Have you ever wondered if the street light outside your house has any effect on the plants which grow in your garden?

We can tell you this: if that light is of the sodium type which gives an orange glow, then the chances are that sweet peas will never flourish.

And if the street is lit by mercury vapour (the purple light which seems to drain all colour from the face), then it is quite likely that geraniums planted nearby will not bloom.

These are facts emerging from experiments into the relationship between plant growth and various types of light which are being conducted at East Grinstead (Sussex) by an American nuclear scientist, Dr. Ron Hubbard.

He tells us that sodium lamps are disliked by all plants because of the "cold" light they produce. These lamps bring out growing plants literally into a cold sweat which can be seen on the foliage.

Mercury vapour is a different proposition. Most plants seem to respond to its light—geraniums excepted.

Dr. Hubbard is already well known to *Garden News* readers. Recently we told you of his experiments with seeds treated by radiation.

Today on the centre pages we bring you exclusive pictures and comments on some of his dramatic achievements, especially those relating to the use of different forms of lighting.

His discovery of a positive yet inexpensive cure for glasshouse mildew will be acclaimed by gardeners and commercial growers everywhere.

The results achieved with treated tomato seed will amaze you.

Dr. Hubbard says his experiments are 25 years ahead of present methods. Read what he is doing and judge for yourselves.

THE DOCTOR SHEDS NEW LIGHT ON MILDEW CURE

ARE YOU PLAGUED WITH MILDEW THAT attacks growing plants under glass?

Do you know what causes it?

Do you know how to prevent it?

Thanks to the dramatic discoveries of nuclear scientist Dr. Ron Hubbard, we can tell you his answers.

THE CAUSE of mildew in greenhouses? None other than the widely recommended use of bottom heat by either electrical or waterpipe systems.

"In twenty years of experimenting I have proved that bottom heat is actually harmful," Dr. Hubbard says. "It is the probable cause of all damp diseases and fungus that attacks so many greenhouses in Winter."

THE CURE for mildew is simple and inexpensive. The doctor's prescription: instal an infra-red ray lamp in your glasshouse like a normal light. "By this method I've discovered how to completely check and prevent the spread of mildew," he proclaims.

This is no idle theorising on Dr. Hubbard's part. At Saint Hill Manor Estate, near East Grinstead in Sussex, we saw enough evidence of his researches to support his assertion that current experiments he is conducting are 25 years in advance of today's methods and ideas.

In his laboratories Dr. Hubbard has developed some brand new ideas based on the relationship of artificial light to plant growth. One experiment involved the growing of tomato plants under different coloured lights. The results were startling.

One interesting point about this particular test of reactions to colours was that under a green light the soil dried out very quickly.

The doctor's explanation is this: "It seems that a green light has some molecular reaction on the water which dries it much quicker than other lights. This could have its own individual application—drying out a house, to give just one example."

What else has been done at Saint Hill Manor?

Recently in *Garden News* Dr. Hubbard claimed he could produce a tomato plant with five times the normal fruit-bearing capacity. THIS HE HAS DONE.

EVER-BEARING

Grown from seeds treated by radiation, plants are growing like vines, are apparently ever-bearing, and each contains 15 trusses with no less than 45 fruits on each truss.

"Seeds from these plants had grown in the same way without any additional treatment by radiation," the scientist told us.

There in the glasshouses, too, is sweet corn that has already grown to 12 feet instead of the usual five feet. The output of corn by each plant is estimated to be five times greater than if grown under normal field conditions.

TREATMENT BY INFRA-RED

Greenhouse owners—and gardeners who grow crops under glass on a commercial scale—will be interested in Dr. Hubbard's assertions that infra-red lights will check mildew and that bottom heat without reasonable lighting is harmful.

Look first at the picture (below). There you see Bert Hall, Grounds Manager at Saint Hill Manor Estate, examining a cucumber which was CURED OF MILDEW by the installation of infra-red lighting.

And above, Dr. Hubbard with a diseased orchid he is treating by exposure to infra-red. A polished tin reflector spreads the light round the greenhouse.

Strip lighting is used in the East Grinstead greenhouse laboratories, but the home gardener need not go to this expense. Infra-red bulbs of 125 watts which fit into ordinary ES lampholders can be bought for eight shillings each.

Two bulbs would be ample for the ordinary greenhouse, Dr. Hubbard says, and as infra-red warms the soil without heating the air, there is no danger of mildew or fungus.

Dr. Hubbard showed us (above) the result of an experiment with watering. The two compartments of the box contain identical plants, the difference being that those in the foreground have received a normal watering while those in the rear have taken the same amount flooded in below the soil. It will be seen that the below-soil group is stronger, and that the soil in the front compartment is drying out more quickly.

ON AND ON THEY GROW

The progress of the tomatoes grown at Saint Hill Manor from seed treated by radiation is clearly seen in plants that have grown to ten feet, with as many as 45 fruits to the truss, with no special feed but just a normal quantity of ammonium sulphate and potash.

And far from being exhausted the tomatoes are making a lot of new growth (see picture top left) and, fruit is forming again on trusses which have already yielded a full quota.

THE LIGHT TEST

Above, you see the results of Dr. Hubbard's research into how tomato plants reacted to coloured lights. Reading from the left the colours used were green, blue, red, yellow and pearl white, each having been placed, together with the plant, inside a sealed box and left for three weeks apart from periodic watering. The healthiest plant grew in yellow light.

The poorest response was to the pearl light but the doctor has proved that plants do respond to clear tungsten bulbs and he advises anyone with indoor plants to use clear and not pearl bulbs in room lights for this reason.

HOW GERANIUMS REACT TO THE LIGHT TEST

So MANY ENQUIRIES FOLLOWED THE RECENT publication in *Garden News* of Dr. Ron Hubbard's research into the connection between street lighting (mercury vapour) and plant growth that we asked the American scientist for further information.

At East Grinstead (Sussex) he has been experimenting with geraniums, raising six identical plants under different types of light. The results you see in the picture above, the key figures denoting:

1   Mercury vapour
2   Clear tungsten bulb
3   Infra-red
4   Ultra-violet
5   Shaded greenhouse
6   Outdoor

Thus it is clear that geraniums have responded best to ordinary tungsten and infra-red lights, these plants being up to a third bigger than the others and flowering well.

The mercury vapour light used on the first plant was an agricultural lamp costing 70s. and used by many commercial growers. Dr. Hubbard says he considers these lamps, besides being expensive and fragile, are less beneficial to plants than the ordinary clear tungsten bulb.

Automating Your Greenhouse

While many a market greenhouse now features automatic irrigation, lighting and temperature control systems, L. Ron Hubbard's original "Horticultural Research Centre" was both a novelty and a wonder. Consequently, and for all else previously reported, Garden News further offered readers the following. ■

Garden News

Friday, February 26, 1960

THIS AUTOMATIC GREENHOUSE USES WARM WATER AT ROOTS

READERS OF *GARDEN NEWS* ARE NOT unfamiliar with the name of Dr. L. Ron Hubbard. We have featured his work and his ideas on several occasions in the past.

We now bring news of an unbelievably simple yet, to our mind, brilliant idea which he has put into practice in the greenhouse of his East Grinstead, Sussex, home.

Basically the idea is to combine three necessary tasks in one simple operation: watering, heating and feeding. And this is the story of how it is done.

In the large picture on the next page you can see—at the foot—a slab which is the lid of a cistern. In this cistern water is heated by means of an immersion heater and it then flows out into a three-inch gravel bed which runs underneath the soil (shown in the diagram on next page). The soil draws up the water, thus heating itself and watering the roots of the plants. And the feed? All you do is pour the feed into the cistern, to mix with the water.

The flow of water is controlled by the ball-cock you can see in both picture and diagram.

The whole house is automatically fitted, by the way. There are automatic controls based on similarly simple ideas, which look after the lighting and air intake, controlled by thermostats and time switches.

Details of the full adaption of the greenhouse are clearly shown in the other pictures on the following pages, but take a tip from this as one immediate result: cucumbers have been planted in the house, and it's enough to say that Dr. Hubbard expects a crop—and they are notoriously difficult to grow in this country in the winter—ready for picking this month.

Over then to another facet of this remarkable set-up. *Garden News* first reported Dr. Hubbard's previous experiments with the effect of light on the growth of plants last year: and his findings are now being confirmed by the pattern of plant growth in the new greenhouse. Three tungsten 200-watt clear bulbs illuminate the greenhouse (which measures 15 ft. × 25 ft.). At first they were switched off for a period during the night.

SHRIVELLED, DISCOLOURED

Now, at that stage, the leaves of the cucumber plants were shrivelled and discoloured and the blooms mildewed off. But when the lights were left on all night, the plants became healthier and the leaves bigger and a fresh green in colour; then as they grew nearer the light so the stalks got thicker and the flowers set. And there was no other change in conditions to account for the improvement.

Another piece of automation: four bowl fires, with infra-red heating elements, are suspended

A sectional view of the automatically controlled greenhouse in which you can see one of the 200-watt tungsten lights in a reflector and one of the infra-red heating elements fitted in a bowl fire reflector. And look at these cucumber plants. There are two advantages in staking them—or tomatoes—this way: greater height in less space and the plant exposed more evenly to the light. Incidentally—in the foreground is the cover to the water cistern. —*Garden News*

from the roof and, by means of a thermostat, keep the air temperature about 75 degrees Fahrenheit.* Then there's a device which enables a constant air temperature to be maintained: this is an air thermostat which is linked to two extraction fans. So what happens? Should the temperature rise above 75 degrees—as it might well do in strong sunshine—the fans suck warm air out of the greenhouse and so draw in fresh air through a louvre at the opposite end of the house, thus lowering the temperature to the required setting.

The net result—apart from the obvious benefit—is that it cuts out the need for opening and closing greenhouse ventilators. In fact, the whole greenhouse "runs itself"—except for tying up the plants as they grow.

Perhaps a robot for this job Dr. Hubbard?

The three controls you can see on the right of the min–max thermometer are the thermostat controlling the infra-red bowl heaters; the on/off switch for the water cistern immersion heater; the time clock controlling the tungsten lights. Above the thermometer is the air thermostat, which controls the two extraction fans (arrowed in the left background), which expel warm air and draw in cool air from a louvre at the other end of the house. —*Garden News*

While 75 degrees Fahrenheit is a serviceable temperature for cucumbers, as previously noted in Ron's memo to the Saint Hill Grounds Manager, a greenhouse is ideally kept substantially warmer.

A close inspection of this picture will show the difference in the two sets of plants. This is another experiment that was carried out to show the difference in growth determined by different water temperatures. Those on the left had a heat of 80 degrees Fahrenheit and those on the right, 65 degrees F. The difference will be even more marked later on. —*Garden News*

NOW—THE ALL-IMPORTANT CONTROLS

This is the primarily simple watering/heating/feeding system—as it appears from above when the feed is being put into the water and—below—as it works shown in a cross section diagram. The incoming water can be controlled by the ball-cock to give any soil condition from swamp to bone-dry, and the speed of the water's circulation is regulated by the use of a pump. Originally, it was left to its own force. Incidentally—it's only too easy to drain the water off by means of a tap in the opposite corner of the house so that it can be refreshed from time to time.

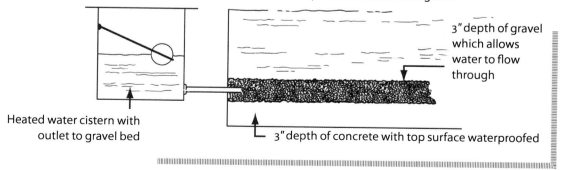

Soil 12" deep absorbs water from gravel

3" depth of gravel which allows water to flow through

Heated water cistern with outlet to gravel bed

3" depth of concrete with top surface waterproofed

AND HERE IS THE FINAL PROOF—THE TEMPERATURE OF WATER-HEATED SOIL

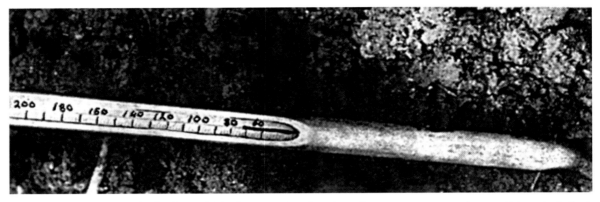

The thermometer gives the final proof. It is shown registering the soil temperature at 73 degrees Fahrenheit. And this is soil heated by the water from below. What more do you want?

Mr. H. D. Hall, Grounds Manager for Dr. Hubbard, is examining one of the cucumber plants. You can see how the lower leaves on the first two or three feet of growth are shrivelled and drooping while from the leaf he is holding the plant is healthier throughout. Why? Because from then on they had the benefit of the tungsten light throughout the night.
—*Garden News*

Sowing and Soil

While only a serious gardener can appreciate the passions perfect soil inspires, suffice it to say here was yet another L. Ron Hubbard discovery sparking banner headlines: his scientific examination of time-honored English peat moss, leaf mold, manure, etc. As Saint Hill tests bore out, and as corroborated decades later, peat indeed proved inadequate. It was no trivial matter, particularly given English reliance on peat moss mixed with sand and fertilizer for practically every plant in the kingdom. So, yes, it would seem only concerted horticulturists could appreciate the passions ignited when the Saint Hill Manor Research Centre condemned moss as a compost failure. Nevertheless and as later corroborated by American agriculturists, peat indeed proved inadequate and actually tended to acidify soil. Thus the Garden News report on L. Ron Hubbard's "quest for the perfect soil medium." ▪

PROOF THAT PEAT MOSS IS A FAILURE AS A COMPOST

The story behind this picture is that leaf mould is a quality compost, whereas peat moss, other than for carrots, is a surprising failure. The two comparisons are taken from soil experiments being carried out by Dr. L. Ron Hubbard at his Sussex Research Station, where he is growing five representative types of vegetable in eight different soil mediums. For the full story, turn to the following page. —*Garden News*

FROM BEHIND THE SERENE FRONT OF THE MANOR COME THESE NEW FINDINGS

POT TEST FOR THE PERFECT SOIL

MORE EXCITING EXPERIMENTS HAVE BEEN revealed by American scientist, Dr. L. Ron Hubbard in his quest for a perfect soil medium.

In the research laboratory of his Sussex country home, Saint Hill Manor, he has just completed the first stage of his tests with eight different soil mediums and five plants, representative of the groups vegetable, vine, corn and root crops.

"We want to find what constitutes the perfect growing soil which will take a plant to maturity—not just a rooting or potting medium," explained Dr. Hubbard's Grounds Manager, Mr. H. D. Hall.

Eight large pots were filled with the eight elements and seed of the selected vegetables.

GARDEN SOIL	SHARP SAND	LEAF MOULD	NEW LEAVES
8 POINTS	21 POINTS	23 POINTS	11 POINTS

As can be seen from our pictures, the different results were remarkable. Seeds planted in old leaves (see pot six) produced the best quality all-round growth.

Right at the bottom, as might be expected, was fresh manure (pot two) but old farmyard manure (pot one) came second to leaf mould for good growth.

AND THE NEXT STAGE?... The two or three best elements will be mixed with soil, separately and in various combinations, and similar tests will continue until the ideal compound is perfected.

PEAT MOSS	GRASS MOWINGS	FRESH MANURE	OLD MANURE
8 POINTS	11 POINTS	6 POINTS	22 POINTS

Eight different soil mediums were selected and into each pot went seed of five representative vegetables: cucumber, pea, carrot, sweet corn and lettuce. The results can be seen at a glance. —*Garden News*

On Germination Rates

Eventually, and expressly to field requests from inquiring journalists, L. Ron Hubbard welcomed one Derek H. Shuff as administrative aide and publicity manager. In such capacity Mr. Shuff provided both general information letters and breaking horticultural news. In this case, Dr. Hubbard's answer to that perennial subject of gardening woe: "Why is the germination rate of seeds so poor?" ∎

Saint Hill Manor Horticultural Research Centre

New Sowing Technique for Improved Germination

Why is the germination rate of seeds so poor? Gardeners are always asking this question.

Is it bacteria? Is it rotting of the seeds by excess water? Or is it just plain bad sowing technique?

At Saint Hill Manor Horticultural Research Centre, Dr. L. Ron Hubbard has achieved a high rate of germination by a new sowing technique.

Four separate beds were used. In two of them soil was carefully prepared, nutrients were added, leaf mould mixed in. Then seeds were laid to a depth of half an inch (as recommended) and covered with soil. In the second two beds the ground was broken up a little and levelled, before the same variety of seeds were scattered over the surface. A quarter inch "mat" of leaf mould was laid on top. No soil was added.

The beds were watered and trodden down a little to keep the leaf mould firm. That was that. Dr. Hubbard refers to the second way as the "lazybones" method.

During the following two days both pairs of beds were watered regularly and this is where the fault in the accepted sowing technique began to reveal itself.

In the conventional bed the surface soil became as hard as a bone. The fibrous compost beneath the surface soil drained what water it contained away—this left a solid crust of upper soil. The dehydrating fibrous matter beneath literally "choked" the seeds to death.

Few seeds managed to germinate, and those that did were retarded in growth.

In the "lazybones" method the beds were covered in a carpet of healthy seedlings within a few days. No chemical foods had been added to the soil, no drills had been made, no special routine followed, and yet germination rate was very high and quick. The leaf mould will supply sufficient food to the growing plants to allow them to grow to maturity, and the fibrous qualities of the compost will retain the necessary moisture.

Try it and see!

The Press Officer
Hubbard Communications Office
Saint Hill Manor,
East Grinstead,
Sussex

Left Beds for sowing experimentation, 1960

The First Crop of 1960

"What may prove to be a revolution in horticultural production is taking place in nurseries in Britain," or so reported papers on the heels of a Saint Hill sweet corn crop from the spring of 1960. That news of it sparked headlines in the East Grinstead Courier is hardly surprising. But in light of startling agrotechnology spurring unprecedented growth rates, word of it ultimately spread internationally. ■

Cornstalks maturing several months in advance of "the season," Saint Hill Manor, 1960

East Grinstead Courier

May 20, 1960

FIRST SWEET CORN CROP RAISED

THE "FIRST SWEET CORN CROP OF 1960" has been grown in the plant research laboratories of Dr. L. Ron Hubbard, of Saint Hill.

Maturing in mid-May instead of the usual August, the crop consists of 169 sweet corn stalks bearing heavy cobs. This is probably the earliest any such crop ever has been grown in England.

Dr. Hubbard specialises in "making plants do the impossible or unexpected." The research activity aims at developing new crops for the British home food supply.

"Sweet corn has difficulty growing in England at all," he said, "and I didn't think this one would be up before late June."

Many Hubbard developments have been the subject of National Press stories.

Advice and Diagnosis

It was a distinctive feature of L. Ron Hubbard's character to encourage participation of others in whatever he himself found productive or enjoyable. The examples are many and span all activities in which he was expert: the arts, aviation, yachting and—as evident from the to-and-fro letters that follow—horticulture. What is presented here represents but a small sampling of correspondence crossing his desk in the wake of what took root at Saint Hill. Also included is the original Garden News notice formally inviting involvement from readers. ∎

Garden News

Friday, April 8, 1960

SCIENTIST SEEKS YOUR HELP IN HIS RESEARCH

GARDEN NEWS READERS ARE, BY NOW, familiar with the research work of Dr. L. Ron Hubbard at East Grinstead in Sussex. A number of the useful results he has achieved have been published in this paper—only last week we announced his claims when testing different types of soil.

Now, Dr. Hubbard has asked *Garden News* readers to join in his experiments with him and to play their part in furthering scientific horticultural knowledge. He would like to hear from any reader who has any ideas on the scientific checking of traditional theories.

Is there anything you have known of for years and which you have wondered, from time to time, if it is in fact correct? If there is—join in. You may be instrumental in bringing to light some great new fact or in destroying faith in some useless practice.

Take this recent case of the basic tests that we announced last week. How many people realised until then that sand is a first-class humus for lettuce, carrots, sweet corn and peas while fresh manure is about the worst?

With the co-operation of *Garden News* readers, Dr. Hubbard could prove or disprove any suggestions that you make.

18 St. Andrews Rd.
Coventry.
20.11.59.

Dear Dr. Hubbard,

I read recently in "Garden News" a short synopsis of your work in the greenhouse—using infra-red light.

I wrote to the editor for further information and he referred me to you. I hope you will not consider this letter a presumption.

I think if I let you know why I am interested in this subject it will help you to give me the necessary information with the minimum of trouble for yourself.

I grow tuberous-rooted begonias and suffer from two common troubles:

1. Black Stem Rot

This starts as a dark patch on the stem and, if left a day or two, gets covered with white spores similar in appearance to mildew.

My foremost treatment—cut away the rot, dry with a cloth and treat with "Orthocide." This works well if the rot is high up on the plant, but as often happens, especially in the Autumn, the rot starts near the tuber. Then, indeed, you are up against it.

2. Cuttings—rotten from the bottom

Stem cuttings planted in cutting compost and the pots kept in warm moist heat (bottom heat). Soaked when planted and left void of water for at least 3 or 4 weeks. Far too many lost by rotting from the bottom.

Is infra-red going to help me with these problems?

If so, how shall I install it and how use it?

Thank you in anticipation.

I Remain

Yours Truly
O. T. Hall MR.
SAE Enclosed

L. Ron Hubbard

Saint Hill Manor,
East Grinstead,
Sussex.

25th November, 1959.

O. T. Hall, Esq.,
18, St. Andrews Road,
COVENTRY,
Warwickshire.

Dear Mr. Hall,

Thank you for your letter of 20th November.

You do not say whether you grow your begonias in large glasshouses, cucumber type houses or just use pots in a covered shed. Therefore at this stage I can only suggest that you take a 250 watt infra-red reflector bulb, instal this about 4 feet above your pots or boxes and give it a trial run for about four weeks. Leave the bulb burning night and day. If it proves successful, further bulbs could be installed in a line 6 feet apart.

Yours truly,
L. Ron Hubbard.

Bryn
Woodcote Rd
Forest Row
Sussex.

3 June 60.

Dear Sir,

For some time I have been interested in the reports of your work. Recently my father, who is editorial secretary of the Soil Association, has written to me to see if I can help him. He has been receiving your Information Sheets, and would like to know more.

Would it be possible for me to come to Saint Hill to see some of your work?

Unfortunately I am not usually free until after 4 p.m. each day, but I have a week's holiday after Whitsun.

Yours faithfully,
O. C. Jenks

Saint Hill Manor,
East Grinstead,
Sussex.

Woodcote Road,
Forest Row,
Sussex.

9th. June '60.

Dear Mr. Jenks,

Dr. Hubbard has asked me to thank you for your letter of June 3rd.

You are certainly welcome to visit Saint Hill, but I would suggest that from the point of view of gardening experiments (in which you stated you are interested) there is little we can show you at this time.

May I suggest that you wait until the end of the Summer, by which time we hope to have special X-ray equipment installed for the purpose of obtaining seed mutations. I'm sure this would interest you.

Yours faithfully,
Derek H. Shuff.
(for Dr. Hubbard).

L. Ron Hubbard

Saint Hill Manor,
East Grinstead,
Sussex.

7th June, 1960.

N. W. Hudson, Esq.,
Senior Research Engineer,
Federal Department of Conservation and Extension,
P.B. 4,
MAZOE,
Southern Rhodesia.

Dear Mr. Hudson,

Thank you for your letter of 28th May. I was most interested to hear from you.

The primary point in moisture, no matter what phase, is setting a constant, or constant cycle of no wide width plus or minus, and maintaining this constant. A somewhat incorrect moisturization is less important than keeping moisturization as near constant as possible.

This conclusion was evolved by many experiments with sweet corn and it was concluded that any moisturization that one could maintain, as a constant, produced less disease and more growth than an "optimum" moisture, drainage, air humidity held not constant for the period of growth, flowering and fruiting of many plants.

I am sorry I have not fully transcribed notes into a paper on this, but I have had much to do. The above conclusion, treated as a theory by you, can be re-established again as a conclusion if you care to check it.

Do write me again if I can be of any further help.

Sincerely,
L. Ron Hubbard

Right With Grounds Manager, 1959

Southville Salons,
62a Ramsgate Road,
Margate,
Kent.

23. 6. 60.

Dear Sir,

I note that you state your willingness to conduct experiments in the growing of plants during this part of the season.

I specialise in chrysanthemums and grow 130 lates and 220 earlies for exhibition.

Would you please let me have your experience of systemic insecticides, notably **TRITOX**, as this is available to amateurs.

Past experience or future knowledge will help, as I am convinced that no sprayed insecticide will get far enough into the growing tip of the plants to eradicate the breeding ground of the aphis.

I have written to several big exhibitors and also spoken to many on the subject, but apparently none of them have the nerve to try the systemics out on our prize stuff, and the journals seem loath to mention them also.

I note that the Garden News has a page in this week's issue on insecticides, but no mention is made of anything other than spraying types.

Hoping for your most valued assistance on this matter.

I remain,
Yours sincerely.
S. J. Foster.

P.S. I have heard that some farmers and commercial growers that use the more powerful systemics find that they cause a break of colour in some cases and these points are the things I would like explained or rejected.

L. Ron Hubbard

S. J. Foster, Esq.,
Southville Salons,
62a Ramsgate Road,
Margate, Kent.

27th. June '60.

Dear Mr. Foster,

Thank you for your enquiry concerning the handling of aphides on chrysanths.

The U.S. long-range commercial method of controlling aphides is the aphis-eating "ladybird" (U.S. "ladybug") bought and released in the houses, with no sprays. This is long-range control for chrysanths ("mums" in the U.S.) and roses, with heavy house sterilization at season's beginning.

Your question concerning a preparation known as Tritox I cannot answer, as I seldom express an opinion on commercial preparations.

However, I feel your problem is easy to solve. The thing with aphides is to start early, before any sign appears to the amateur. Sterilize the area before cultivation and, using any common spray or vapour or wash, keep the plants clean of insects and disease.

In choosing a sterilizer for an empty house, use something strong. In the soil of an empty house, use some weak creosote derivative, watered in with a sprinkling can, not sprayed.

Then when the plants are young, use a weak spray or vapour that will not injure the plants or wilt them but will stop the larvae. The oldest remedy is paraffin emulsion.

However, are you sure your chrysanthemums are being attacked by aphides and not chrysanthemum leaf miner? The oldest remedy for this is paraffin emulsion.

Any vapour or insecticide as a commercial product has to be tried on its own merits. I would not develop any reverence for these, untried. They are usually based on commonly available materials.

Your problem is not one that will be solved by a special spray or preparation so much as one that requires an *early* address before the problem appears. Do that, and, providing the growing of the plant is good, you will have no later worries.

Sterile house, sterile soil and weak spraying at early intervals resolve most insect and pest problems. Outside, sterile soil and spraying regularly with weak preparations on windless days over a longer period will keep any insect problems at bay.

Yours sincerely,
L. Ron Hubbard.

JAMES CARTWRIGHT.

65, REGINALD RD

BEARWOOD

SMETHWICK,

STAFFS

18-7-60

Dear Sir,

CHRYSANTHEMUMS

On seeing in the Garden News you are willing to help anyone with their troubles and problem, I would like to take this chance, hoping you can help me. We've been growing chrysanthemums for a few years now, but like many more growers I am finding it getting more trouble each year, keeping my stock free from disease. The new varieties that come out every few years seem more liable to be affected. Each year I purchase around a hundred plants and on the last three seasons I had the bad luck to find some of my plants go down with something attacking the foliage. I hate to think it, but the way the leaves go brown and dry up, it seems to me that there may be cutworm. We have sprayed them twice and it seems to have checked the upward spread of drying leaves. Also, I have two plants that I think are suffering with stunt virus, but you may find the real trouble for me. I hope so. My soil is very light and soon dries out. All the waste compost from old pots are put on at the end of the year and I dress my soil with Basic Slag, 4 oz. per square yard in winter, and then, in April, 4 oz. of bone meal, 4 oz. of Bentley early flowering fert. per square yard and plant out in May. Last year, the plants that were affected, the blooms were also distorted and colours pale. Hoping you can help me. Thank you.

TOMATOES

Just another problem. Being a reader of the Gardens News, I was interested in the columnist's reports each week on tomatoes. He stated that sulphate of iron is very good to keep a check on tomato mildew, used at the rate of 1/4 oz. per gallon of water and sprayed on the plants. I had the mildew last year, so I thought this would help me. But to my horror, the next day after spraying late at night, I found the leaves brown and also the stems and tomatoes were covered with black specks. It was almost like thick oil. It did not stop the plants growing, but I cannot get the speck off the tomatoes. I was wondering if you can tell me if there is anything wrong with the iron. I am sending you a sample to see what you think is wrong with it, if anything. Would you think the solution is too strong for the plants? Also, I am enclosing some almond skins, which we use for standing the paper rings on what we grow in. We put about a six-inch layer down and plant on the tomatoes in the ring. I have been wondering if there is any acid in them to have effect on the soil for when I put a covering on the beds of outdoor chrysanthemums. It seems very strange to me that we never have any weeds come growing up through them. I must say, at the end of the season when the tomatoes are taken out of the house, these skins just roll up into a fine peat and we use it for potting soil the following year. Well, I will close now hoping you can help me, if there is any charge or fee, let me know. Thank you very much.

I remain yours.
J. CARTWRIGHT.

L. Ron Hubbard

Saint Hill Manor,
East Grinstead,
Sussex.

22nd July '60.

65, Reginald Road
Bearwood,
Smethwick,
Staffs.

Dear Mr. Cartwright,

I received your box of plants and letter and will let you know more about the diseases when I've looked up my records or done some work on your specimens.

This is certainly a disease year. Insects, weeds and mold are very heavy, due for the most part to excessive cloudiness, cold and rain. Lack of sun is closely connected with mildew, black spot and other diseases. Cloche growing, mineralizing the soil with trace elements, gentle spraying, usually add up to better control of the ills of plants.

But this year has been a rough one so far for everything but weeds! And of course grass, shrubs and trees.

As I see it older strains of tomatoes, chrysanths are wearing down. And in a bad wet year they don't hold up well against disease. I am trying my hand at some new strains. I have a new strain of tomatoes in development that is staying healthy despite the upsets attacking older strains nearby. They were artificially mutated. I am going to try to develop some new chrysanths by soft radiation. And also some pinks. I hope to develop several new flowers that grow well even in a wet, cloudy summer.

Later

Having done a test on brown spots, I checked recent spray tests on potato sprays and note the following: About 3 weeks *after* the spraying, that part of the crop that had been sprayed collapsed, developed brown spots and rotted. The part that was *not* sprayed, though attacked by insects, stayed healthy. A week later the unsprayed portion is still thriving and recovered from the insects, though not sprayed. As nothing else was done to this test, on a "series of one on potatoes," it could be that advised insect and mildew sprays, two weeks after application, cause a plant to become "diseased." The product you named was the insect spray used in this test, exactly according to directions! Another test of this spray on cucumbers under glass produced the same effect. Another test affected colored leaf plants. Another test of it produced brown spots on begonias or killed all their leaves.

Having now looked all this up in my notes on tests here, it appears likely that the spray you used or are using could be weakening down your tomatoes and chrysanths. Your specimens compare with the test specimens here.

So far as I am concerned, this closes your case. Return to older or different much more gentle insect and mildew sprays, get more mineral (trace elements) in your soil and put up a windbreak on outside plots that don't obstruct the sun.

Best,
L. Ron Hubbard

Methods of Transplanting

Quite in addition to all Ron directed within his famed Saint Hill greenhouse lay the fifty-five acres of surrounding manor parkland where he further supervised care of gardens and trees. For a glimpse of it, Saint Hill staff still tell of the morning they found the man sweeping branch-cracking snow from a famed Cedar of Lebanon (reputed to be one of England's finest, and a tree of which Ron was especially fond). Also reflective of his keen arboreal interest was his development of new transplanting methods as reported in the following article from October 1960. ■

The long-loved Cedar of Lebanon, originally planted circa 1710 and reputed to be among the finest in all England

Garden News

October 1960

TRY THIS NEW WAY OF TRANSPLANTING TREES

A QUESTION OF PROVIDING WATER FOR THE ROOTS

HAVE YOU HAD TROUBLE WITH transplanted trees? If so, why not abandon the recommended methods on the next occasion and try a new idea thought up by Dr. L. Ron Hubbard, of Saint Hill Manor Horticultural Research Centre near East Grinstead, Sussex. Dr. Hubbard believes that it gives the tree a 100 per cent chance of healthy survival.

You start—not unusually—by digging a hole, say two feet deep by 15 inches wide (naturally the size of the hole will depend on the size of the tree to be transplanted) making sure the roots fall in comfortably. Before inserting the tree, place a piece of black, or clear, polythene to form a "cup" at the bottom of the hole, and fill this with small rounded pebbles. Do not use sharp stone by the way, for this will pierce the polythene.

Down one side of the hole lean a bamboo rod, one end resting in the pebbles, the other end just protruding above the ground surface.

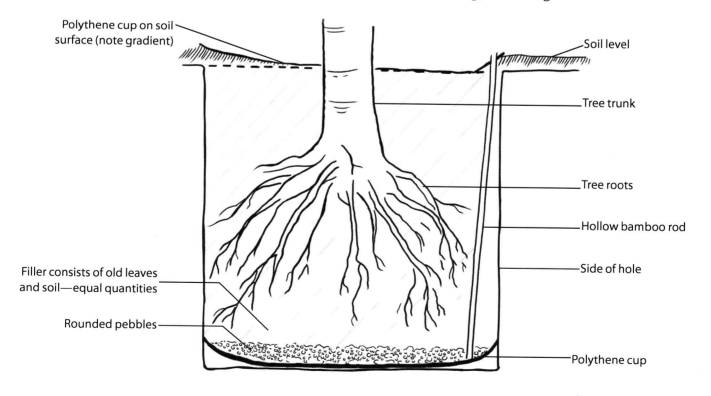

Polythene cup on soil surface (note gradient)

Soil level

Tree trunk

Tree roots

Hollow bamboo rod

Side of hole

Filler consists of old leaves and soil—equal quantities

Rounded pebbles

Polythene cup

Now place in the tree. Pack the "filler" firmly, but carefully, using a composition of old leaves and soil (equal quantities).

Level off the surface allowing a slight gradient towards the top end of the bamboo stick and then cut another piece of black polythene to form another cup round the tree and the bamboo stick.

The idea is this: the rain drains down the tree trunk into the polythene cup—from here it continues down the hollow bamboo rod to the basin at the roots where it is most required. The pebbles will help store the water for the roots.

The black polythene on the ground surface attracts and conserves the heat and also allows the tree to grow and expand normally free from weeds, at the same time preventing rain from packing the earth too tightly near to the surface.

As the young tree adapts itself to its new surroundings the plastic bowl will be obliterated by the penetrating roots, but when this does happen, the tree will have settled down to a healthy and natural growth. The roots will no longer require the water the bowl provided.

CHAPTER TWO

Advanced
EXPERIMENTATION

Advanced Experimentation

T HE CENTRAL PRACTICE OF SCIENTOLOGY IS CALLED *auditing.* It comprises a unique form of spiritual counseling wherein an individual is helped toward greater awareness and abilities through an examination of his own life and existence. Auditing is delivered by an auditor (from the Latin *audire,* "one who listens") and employs highly precise procedures in a highly precise fashion. The auditor is aided by a specially designed meter known as an Electropsychometer, or E-Meter, which measures an individual's state or change of state. Thus an E-Meter detects the otherwise hidden sources of spiritual trauma and travail auditing addresses. Yet following from axiomatic truths of Scientology wherein all life becomes an intrinsically spiritual process, the E-Meter was found capable of detecting other things.

The central proposition was simple enough: if all living things are indeed directed by a spiritual life energy that is distinct and separate from the material universe, then how did one categorize the various *types* of life? That is, did the plant kingdom represent an entirely different order of life from either animal life or human life? Or, conversely, did the whole of life factually represent a single spectrum wherein every living thing responded to stimuli in much the same way? In answer to those questions and more, Ron tells of designing a series of experiments to actually measure the postulated life energy of plants.

Procedural details are equally easy to grasp. The electrodes of an E-Meter emit an imperceptible electrical flow capable of registering minute changes in mental energy and/or reactions to stimuli. Thus although plants may not actually "think," even an infinitesimal response to stimuli would theoretically trigger a needle movement on the meter dial—*and so it did.*

"The accurate scientific statement is a plant injured generates the same wavelengths as a man injured," Ron explained. Yet even the least scientifically minded publications were

An iconic image of that pivotal moment when plants were found to generate wavelengths akin to all other living things

not slow to grasp the ramifications of what the E-Meter disclosed.

To cite but one: "With this meter it is possible to tell, for instance, if plants or vegetables are ever likely to make the local flower show and, having got there, qualify for a prize. This is a simple example and only a fractional illustration of its many uses. In short, if we were to organize on a large scale the scientific and psychological knowledge gained through such experiments as those being carried out by Dr. Hubbard, we could in this present decade alone revitalize the world's food resources and increase our supplies to such abundance that no man, woman or child, even in the remotest areas of the world, need ever again go without an adequate meal."

Consequently and in reasonably short order, Dr. Hubbard received requests for information/notices of corollary studies from half a dozen

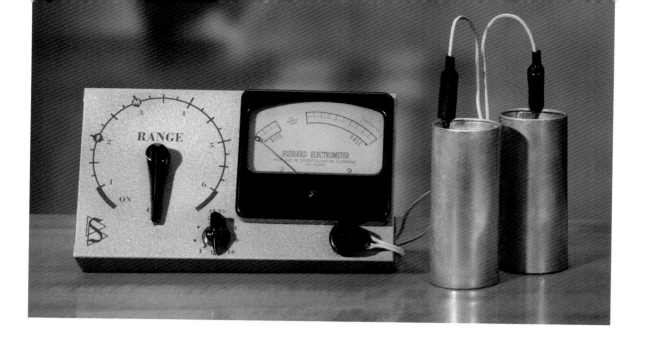

Above
A first transistorized Electropsychometer, or E-Meter: this was the instrument with which Ron unearthed the secrets of plant life

institutions—quite literally from the Israeli Ministry of Commerce to the United States Department of Agriculture.

It was also at this juncture a "most likeable and confident" Dr. Hubbard ushered millions into his experimental laboratory via British television. Meanwhile the Sunday supplements proclaimed: "Revolution rocks the plant kingdom!" and "Never in all the eons since the first green leaf poked its head out of the Paleozoic swamp have plants created such a stir as they have during the past year." Whereupon L. Ron Hubbard's horticultural revelations indeed assumed global prominence and thereafter continued sparking articles and derivative studies for decades to come.

That all such experimentation ran in tandem with all other horticultural investigation is once more significant. For the fact is Ron's examination into the emotional life of plants *cannot* be divorced from all other factors bearing on plant vitality. Thus what follows here must be viewed as both chronologically and scientifically *parallel* to all else.

Finally, while various statements through subsequent newspaper reports are not, strictly speaking, accurate—Ron, for example, never categorically described plants as either thinking or suffering—the fundamental proposition is now common ground across the whole of the horticultural landscape. That is, and most succinctly:

"I found that we must have a better communication with plants, if we are ever to begin to understand them and use them to the fullest advantage of Mankind." ∎

The Inner Life of Plants Revealed

As an opening word on findings from L. Ron Hubbard's advanced horticultural experimentation stands his own summary statement of discoveries. That the statement includes a definition of organic disease as ultimately rooted in mental/spiritual trauma is more than a little significant. Indeed, here is where L. Ron Hubbard's horticultural discoveries grow truly transcendent; for here is that intersection between discoveries enhancing survival of plants and the greater body of Dianetics and Scientology for enhancing survival of all humankind. Here is also an application of Scientology principles for calming horticulturists themselves—and thus those who, as Ron describes, actually produce living things. The paper dates from June 1959 and is published here for the first time. ■

SUMMARY OF ADVANCED EXPERIMENTATION

by L. RON HUBBARD

I HAVE CONDUCTED A TEST showing that plants suddenly bereft of a stem or a top experience a galvanic shock of a traumatic nature.

Earlier tests showed that a plant's freedom from disease was proportional to its willingness to grow.

It is highly probable that freedom from disease is almost entirely dependent upon a congenial atmosphere and attitude (food, moisture, light, heredity).

Any heavy suppression of the impulse to survive apparently causes a desire to die, expressed in a plant's cooperation with things seeking to kill it.

A plant will rise somewhat to an emergency or shock and surge to survive. But shortly there is an abandonment of survival if the suppression is repeated or continued. Thus a shock produces an upsurge toward further survival and, if repeated, invites death.

Traumatic shock can be experienced by a plant is what I have basically demonstrated.

Commercial growers see the effect of administering shock in surging of growth by snipping tops, leaves, etc., but they do not see the side effects of disease as due to the shocks.

Until we see otherwise, we will use this theory and follow these general rules:

1. We will omit the commercial surgery practices on plants;

2. We will supply light in ratio to heat and humidity;

3. We will supply heat and humidity in ratio to light;

4. We will choose disease-resistant strains;

Saint Hill Manor greenhouse

5. We will avoid heavy sprays and disease-killers injurious to the plants as well as the disease;

6. We will avoid transplantings wherever possible and when we do we will use methods to protect fully root systems as with cups;

7. We will sterilize soil and houses with gases or heavy heat or electric currents which leave no aftereffect and do it *before* we commercially plant any house;

8. We will avoid barnyard fertilizers;

9. We will use clean chemicals and careful balances of minerals;

10. If a house dries out accidentally or has a heavy mechanical failure, we will use our judgment whether to continue its plants or sweep it out and start with new plants (dependent on how close the crop is to fruiting);

11. We will be careful not to hire and will weed out very heavy-footed help that damages plants continually while working around them;

12. We will try to take any fruit, yield or bloom with minimum shock and at the end of fruiting rather than repeatedly while fruiting;

13. We will not grow things that are particularly susceptible to injury in handling.

If we do these things and prevent chilling, drying and darkening, we may be able to have that rare thing, a commercial enterprise comparatively free of bugs and blights.

Note: Another test showed that commercial growers have a reactive attitude toward plants, expressed in an impulse always to be doing things to them, whether necessary or unnecessary. This obsessive doingness is what adds all the peculiar "necessary steps" that you find in their manuals.

With this there is another attitude, one of abuse, stemming from worry over economics and demands on the plants to produce "before the overdraft is called in." Where a grower has had many failures, he sometimes begins to take it out on the plants for revenge, unconsciously indulging in active-destructive actions as though they were people or were to blame or were plotting to bankrupt him.

Heavy produce can be commercially secured by speeding growth while watering, feeding and lighting adequately, but all efforts to shock plants into production are apparently also productive of side effects such as disease and poor quality.

The continuous outflow of product to market without much inflow could also produce a non-optimum mental attitude by a grower which would make his attitude toward his product a little queer. In Scientology this is called a "stuck flow" (stuck because it goes only one way too long). Therefore the opinions, attitudes and practices of commercial growers in general are not a good guide to successful commercial growing of produce.

(A trick that would overcome the "stuck flow" would be to have the operation's trucker always bring back a box or two of fancy produce for the boss and the workers whenever a load of produce went to market. The produce brought back would be scrounged from wholesalers' surpluses and bought at low prices. Also some small amount of the produce grown should be given to the people who work in the establishment. So long as this did not injure the economic picture of the grower's establishment to any degree, it would be found to repay itself many times over in terms of better working attitude, resulting in less plant destruction.)

Cooperation with the survival reactions of living things, as covered in Scientology, when understood and handled, produces *living* things.

Revolution Rocks the Plant Kingdom!

The sheer wonder and amazement with which the world responded to L. Ron Hubbard's Advanced Experimentation still marks an astonishing chapter in horticultural history. That many a banner headline was unashamedly sensational is altogether beside the point. Plants were no longer emotionless and insentient. On the contrary, they were alive in the most meaningful sense of the word; while consequent to that, and reflected in a myriad of articles from across every continent, imaginations soared. ■

East Grinstead Courier

Friday, September 25, 1959

CAN PLANTS THINK? HE ASKS

At Saint Hill Manor, East Grinstead, where the seasons are reversed and traditional gardening has been receiving a few hefty jolts, the most amazing experiment has been carried out. It leaves one asking, "Do plants think?"

Dr. L. Ron Hubbard, the American nuclear physicist, whose researches in plant life at the Manor look like he is revolutionising horticulture, has carried out an experiment which points to the fact that plants react in much the same way to certain situations as do human beings.

He has made this discovery by using a super-sensitive device, called an Electropsychometer (or E-Meter), which he designed for use in Scientological work.

When the two electrodes on the E-Meter are held by a person the emotional reaction to questions is recorded. In particular it has proved the consistent human response to the suggestion of death.

GUINEA PIGS

When Dr. Hubbard was tracing the nerve system of plants, just for amusement, he attached the electrodes to a tomato plant. The needle started to register a reaction, and when he pulled off a shoot the needle started to "hunt"—normal reaction to death in a human being.

This week a *Courier* reporter and a photographer acted as "guinea pigs" in a session on the E-Meter, and then saw it carried out on a tomato plant.

The results were fantastic—as fantastic as the thought that plants might be able to think and feel. If this is true it is going to have the most far-reaching effect on vegetarians, it seems.

Also at Saint Hill, Dr. Hubbard is successfully raising plants from seeds normally planted in the Spring. He is growing them in an outdoor bed under an infra-red lamp.

DAY AND NIGHT

All the seeds—sweet corn, cucumbers, radish, pole-beans, peas, carrots, tomatoes and tobacco—have germinated and are growing strongly.

The light, which burns day and night, presented a problem because it attracted a multitude of bugs, but that has been overcome by painting the inside of the light cover with a strong solution of orchard DDT.

The Kingdom of Plants Revealed! In the wake of L. Ron Hubbard's horticultural discoveries, upwards of five million British readers—a full thirty million globally—were suddenly transfixed by revelations from the vegetal world and visions of gardens alive with passion.

Daily Mirror

Dr. RON PLANTS FOOD FOR THOUGHT

I WENT down to the wilds of Sussex yesterday to meet a remarkable, bewildering American scientist—red-haired, forty-eight-year-old Dr. L. Ron Hubbard. He is dedicated to the proposition that plants can

The Washington Star
WASHINGTON, D.C.

New methods for growing out-of-season plants

WHAT MAY PROVE to be a revolution in horticultural production is taking place in nurseries in Britain and other countries, writes a correspondent of "The Times."

GARDEN NEWS
FRIDAYS   FOURPENCE

PLANTS DO WORRY AND FEEL PAIN

A DISCOVERY of immense significance to all gardeners has been made by American nuclear scientist Dr. L. Ron Hubbard, whose experiments at East Grinstead (Sussex) with the effect of light on plants have been related recently in *Garden News*.

New and better, he believes, will be possible by

Evening Citizen

When 2 tomatoes fall in love...

The geranium that for the past year had stood in the window of a parlour in a Glasgow backwater had claustrophobia—tired of being cooped up in its pot. The tomato plant from an Airdrie greenhouse was psychotic. The carrots from a Hamilton garden, the cabbages from Motherwell, the beetroot from Strathaven—all had a neurosis.

Reveille

THE FRIGHTENED TOMATO

I've never troubled to think...

Lilliput

THE SEX LIFE OF A VIRILE CABBAGE

GARDEN NEWS
FRIDAYS FOURPENCE

Dr Hubbard seen by TV millions

This Week
— M A G A Z I N E —

Are Plants "Human"?
Revolution rocks the plant kingdom!

CAN PLANTS THINK? YES, SAYS A NUCLEAR PHYSICIST!

Dr. L. Ron Hubbard, American nuclear physicist, uses an Electropsychometer (or E-Meter) to demonstrate his theory that plants can think *and suffer*. First he shows his machine registering the reaction of fear and emotion on a man. Then he connects it to a growing tomato, and adjusts it until it registers the presence of living matter. Suddenly he thrusts a nail through the tomato skin...the needle quivers, the machine registers what in man would be "an indication of extreme anxiety and fear of death" says Dr. Hubbard, who is convinced this proves that the plant can think and anticipate ultimate danger to its own life.

Main purpose of the experiment is to try to read the state of mind of plants, keep them "happy" and thereby increase the world's food supply. Dr. Hubbard finances all his own research, and has recently settled in East Grinstead where he has established a laboratory.

Yet another profusion of global headlines inspired by reports of L. Ron Hubbard's discoveries at Saint Hill—this one replete with anthropomorphic images of distressed vegetables

June 26, 1960

This Week
MAGAZINE

Are Plants "Human"?

TORONTO DAILY STAR

TUESDAY, JULY 5, 1960   PAGES 25 TO 40

"BUT I SHAVED THIS MORNING"

"HONEST, MR. CASTRO, IT WASN'T US WHO BOOED"

She Bit...

"OKAY, TOMORROW I START THAT DIET"

"HONEY, WHERE'D YOU PUT THE SUNBURN LOTION?"

Listen to the Salad Symphony

... and the Peach Screamed

electronometer is connected to any fruit or vegetable Hubbard wishes to
t records the normally inaudible sounds emitted as the subject is sliced,
diced or crushed. Here peach's death rattle is recorded as it is bitten

d these are the
would be most
e to the scientifi
ious processes of

the doctor said, it is possible to tell, for instance,
if flowers or vegetables
are ever likely to win

infra red rays on orchids
or cucumbers can produce
them all year round in
Manhattan or Timbuctoo.

"THAT DARNED INSTANT LATHER COMES OUT TOO FAST"

"FROM NOW ON, NO MORE OFFICE PARTIES FOR ME"

"HOW COULD I KNOW HIS KID HAD THE MEASLES?"   "I JUST WASHED MY HAIR AND CAN'T DO A THING WITH IT"

Farmers' Weekly, South Africa

January 18, 1961

PLANTS CAN WORRY AND FEEL PAIN

A PLANT CAN FEEL PAIN AND "WORRY" IN A way comparable with human thought—this is the startling discovery of an American nuclear physicist working in Britain. The discovery was made recently by Dr. L. Ron Hubbard who lives at East Grinstead in Sussex.

In his experiments, Dr. Hubbard uses a specially sensitive version of the skin galvanometer—an instrument called an Electropsychometer (or E-Meter). The meter measures the densities and flows of the life energy in the body and, by interpreting the readings, the state of thought can be ascertained. It is, therefore, an infallible test of the presence of life.

PRESENCE OF LIFE

In a demonstration given by Dr. Hubbard, he first showed how the emotions of a man, such as fear and guilt, registered on the meter. Then a tomato growing on a plant, was connected to the meter by two contacts. The sensitivity control of the meter was adjusted until the presence of life showed and then a nail was stuck into the tomato.

The needle on the galvanometer dial quivered and began to rise. "The same reading on a man would indicate extreme anxiety and fear of death," Dr. Hubbard said. "This shows that in some way a plant can 'think' and 'worry' about its chances of survival." The meter continued to show a reaction by the plant for some minutes after the nail was pushed in—as would be the case with a human being who suffered a similar shock to his nervous system.

Although the implications of this discovery have still to be evaluated, Dr. Hubbard believes it will give remarkable control over plant growth. For example, he believes it will be possible to select from, say, one thousand plants at the seedling stage, the one which will give, ultimately the finest bloom or fruit. By using this "plant psychology," market garden managers would know exactly how satisfied the plants were with the way the gardeners handled them. Better and hardier varieties of fruit and vegetables could be raised in a fraction of the time it takes today, by assessing the reactions of a plant at an early stage of growth.

In the same way, the future health of a plant could be predicted by reading its "state of mind."

"Plants only catch a disease or blight if they are already thinking of dying," says Dr. Hubbard.

His other experiments at East Grinstead have shown how various types of lighting stimulate or retard plant growth. He has also solved the problem of growing tomatoes all the year round in Britain—hitherto regarded as an impossible commercial proposition—by having an infra-red lamp in the greenhouse, with no other form of heating at all. And by bombarding seeds with X-rays he has produced a crop of tomatoes which have already given five times the normal yield, and are still bearing fruit.

An Insider's View

Providing yet another view of Saint Hill gardening discoveries is Press Agent Derek Shuff's notice to Scientologists. It is predicated on L. Ron Hubbard's compartmentalization of life into eight dynamic urges. That is, the whole of existence may be viewed in terms of eight distinct dynamic drives or impulses. The dynamics extend from an urge to survive as self through an urge to survive through sex and family, groups, all Mankind and more. The Fifth Dynamic pertains to life in general. Thus, on the Fifth Dynamic, an individual strives to help all other living things survive—very much including the plant kingdom. ■

Saint Hill Manor Horticultural Research Centre

Mr. Hubbard's Horticultural Research

You may be asked or may wish to inform people why Dr. Hubbard is doing plant research at all.

Plants are the Fifth Dynamic of Scientology, a logical area of Scientology research.

Since plants are bodies of a sort with a rapid cycle-of-action, Dr. Hubbard has already learned much about human disease by studying plant disease. Some of our recent developments in technology were discovered in plants by Dr. Hubbard.

In studying life and life sources he made a fundamental discovery last fall [1959] that plants are the same order of life form as animals or humans. This opened the door widely to more understanding of life.

His plant research is of great interest in itself. But it is of greater interest to Scientology as providing a more detached look at life than is possible in handling only humans.

Revolutionizing the art of gardening in itself is a probable outcome—and we are well on the way toward it. But this, though interesting, is incidental to the main study of life.

ATOMIC SEEDS

There is a great opening for pioneer research into seed mutation by means of X-rays and other rays. In America Dr. Hubbard carried out research in this line as long ago as he can remember. This makes him a leading authority on "atomic gardening." At Saint Hill Manor he is in the process of setting up special equipment to carry on this valuable work. Word spread round of his interest in atomic gardening, and only last month (in April) Dr. Hubbard was invited, and accepted, a position on the scientific advisory board of the Atomic Gardening Society which meets in London.

He addressed members at one of the Society's meetings in London on April 30th, 1960 and pointed out that by developing strains of certain types of plants, food productivity can be greatly increased throughout the world. By developing certain food-producing plants, such as tomatoes, the quantity of edible matter from each can be increased through mutations. Dr. Hubbard discovered that by bombarding seeds with X-rays their characteristics are changed. At Saint Hill Manor plants have been grown by this method, tomato plants for example, which produced large, hardy and disease-resisting plants, bearing five times the normal amount of fruit that might be expected from an ordinary tomato. This was acclaimed in the British gardening press. Many of you may have read about this.

Here is the type of horticultural work that Dr. Hubbard intends to concentrate upon during the coming summer months.

His address in London made a great impact on those present. This could well be the beginning of great things. How to feed the ever-increasing populations in the world is a problem confronting many governments. It is a heartening thought that a solution is being conceived at Saint Hill Manor by Dr. Hubbard.

The Press Officer
Hubbard Communications Office
Saint Hill Manor,
East Grinstead,
Sussex

Corollary Discoveries

"Every time I saw a research bed of plants worsen, I queried what routine had been varied and found invariably some big change had been made that wasn't usual.

"It is change that changes things for better or for worse. That's the simplicity of the natural law." —LRH

*I*T WAS ALSO THE NATURAL SPRINGBOARD to several L. Ron Hubbard discoveries at least as revolutionary as what he provided horticulture—most notably, a body of administrative discoveries known as the Data Series. Resting on axiomatic principles of Dianetics and Scientology, the Data Series offers the first substantive codification of logic in the last three thousand years. In the simplest terms, it might best be described as a "way of thinking" or a "technology of thinking." It is also a way of viewing events and provides the first regimented procedure for isolating the underlying cause of any non-optimum situation. At its core lie certain irreducible laws monitoring survival potentials and those laws are applicable to all living things and all ventures—administration, organization, business, civics and every form of social interaction. While most popularly the tool of managerial executives, the Data Series is indeed partially rooted in L. Ron Hubbard's horticultural discoveries. The following, then, is drawn from the series itself and dates from 1970. ∎

CHANGE & RECOVERY

by L. RON HUBBARD

IN ORDER TO DETECT, handle or remedy situations, one has to be able to understand and work out several things.

These are defining the Ideal Scene itself, detect without error or guess any departure on it, find out WHY a departure occurred and work out a means of reverting back to the Ideal Scene.

In order to resolve a situation fully, one has to get the *real* reason WHY a departure from the Ideal Scene occurred.

"What was changed?" or "What changed?" is the same question.

That "change" is the root of departures comes from a series of plant experiments I conducted. (The type of experimentation was undertaken to study cellular life behavior and reaction to see if it was a different *type* of life—it isn't. The experiments themselves were later repeated in various universities and were the subject of much press for them over the world.)

In setting up conditions of growth, I observed that plants on various occasions greatly declined suddenly. In each case I was able to trace the last major CHANGE that had occurred and correct it. Changes made in temperature, water volume, humidity, ventilation greatly affected the plants in terms of wilt, decreased growth rate, increase in parasites, etc.

When THE change was isolated and the condition reverted to that occurring during the previous healthy period, a recovery would occur.

At first glance this may seem obvious. Yet in actual practice it was not easy to do.

Gardeners' records would omit vital data or alter importance or drop out time, etc. A gardener might seek to cover up for himself or a fellow worker. He tended to make himself right and would enter falsehoods or reassurance that was a falsehood into the analysis.

A new gardener would seem to affect the plants greatly and one could build a personality influence theory on this—until one found that, being untrained in the procedure used, he would enter even more outpoints than usual.

At such a juncture one would of course train the gardener. BUT that didn't locate WHAT had been changed. And one had to locate that to get the plants to recover. The conditions in use were extreme forcing conditions anyway and lapse of duty was very apparent. Sixteen-foot hothouse American corn from seeds usually furnishing five-foot stocks, forty-three tomatoes to the truss where five is more usual were the demands being met. So any change showed up at once.

The fact of change itself was a vital point as well. One discovery was that life does best in a near optimum constancy—meaning that change just as change is usually harmful to plant life.

The fact of isolating change in the environment as the sole harmful cause was one discovery.

That one had to isolate THE change in order to obtain full recovery was another discovery.

Change itself was not bad, but in this experimental series conditions were set as optimum and the beneficial changes had already been made with remarkable results. Thus one was observing change from the optimum.

This would be the same thing as "departures from the Ideal Scene."

The action was always:

1. Observe the decline.

2. Locate the exact change which had been made.

3. Revert THE change.

4. A return to the near Ideal Scene would occur if one were maintaining the Ideal Scene meanwhile.

CHAPTER THREE

Cultural
OUTGROWTH

Cultural Outgrowth

"IT WOULD SEEM THAT L. RON HUBBARD WAS 10 YEARS ahead of his time." —New Zealand's *Evening Post,* January 1970. It would also seem L. Ron Hubbard was both inspiration and catalyst for much of what the 1970s signaled in the way of a newfound reverence for all living things and a vision of life as an interwoven partnership for survival. In other words and in short, it would seem that what burst into bloom at his Saint Hill laboratory ten years earlier were cultural tendrils winding through and through this civilization.

To cite but a little of the ripple effect: beyond L. Ron Hubbard's horticultural harvest of 1959/1960 came a host of imitative studies. Among the more interesting were conducted at the Moscow Agricultural Academy and suggested plants are actually capable of processing information relative to survival through some form of cognitive mechanism. There was another from the University of Zurich—this one to expressly replicate LRH experimentation and successfully so—while similarly corroborative experimentation in Australia sparked national headlines reading: *"Amazing tests prove plants have feelings!"*

There was appreciably more: in 1966, a former interrogation specialist with the United States Central Intelligence Agency named Cleve Backster claims to have impulsively attached a galvanometer to the leaves of a *Dracaena massangeana.* At which point, and with some vehemence, he summarily concluded: "Plants can think!" That Backster inevitably drew academic fire for not adhering to usual experimental standards is moot. For having earned a mention in a bestselling New Age reader entitled *The Secret Life of Plants,* which by turns inspired a visionary Stevie Wonder album by the same name, so it proliferated and so it lived on.

To cite yet another from the early 1970s: scientific experiments wherein leaves were attached to "sophisticated electronic equipment capable of registering the slightest

"Although scientists have been able to examine the smallest basic constituents of plants under powerful microscopes, scientists have not been able to synthesise these components into a plant. It seems that there are other factors involved beside those that can be seen physically." —South Africa's *Natal Witness,* July 1975. And so it was the central revelation from L. Ron Hubbard's horticultural research of 1959 continued to engender a worldwide parade of press.

The Natal Witness

The oldest newspaper in South Africa — Established 1846

Does talking to plants give improved results?

Feeling ... able to react to their environment. There are many examples of plants that react ...

THE Sun

A love affair with a garden

This seems to me to be a very healthy   with plants and their reactions to us humans   The pen was calmly tracing a line up the

Holyoke Daily Transcript

Tomatoes Should Be Cuddled, Not Sliced

Daily Mirror

Only a rose, but they can feel like humans

The sweet-smelling rose isn't just a pretty face. For that prickly skin hides a tender heart, scientists claimed yesterday.

OTTAWA CITIZEN

THURSDAY   ESTABLISHED IN 1845

Potty or not, some say plants have feelings

LONDON· There's growing feeling   plants are capable of establishing   hooked up to sophisticated electronic

emotional reaction" suggested plants were capable of forming emotional attachments. There was more again to suggest vegetation possessed some form of memory and particularly relative to survival threats. But as repeatedly stressed in various publications and various ways: L. Ron Hubbard was categorically "the first to bluntly state that plants, like humans, can feel pain, worry and anxiety."

And still there was more: "Scientists have been steadily helping agriculture to increase production," announced a British *Farmers Weekly* in 1980 and specifically noted that subsequently confirmed LRH discoveries from twenty years earlier indeed translate into dramatically increased crop yield. While in emphasis thereof came a reprint of original reports from the summer of 1960 when Saint Hill cornstalks stood five times taller than those grown under normal field conditions.

Thus from both hindsight and foresight came the overriding conclusion: *"This type of research could have far-reaching benefits for Mankind."*

"This type of research could have far-reaching benefits for Mankind."

So, yes and unquestionably, what issued forth from L. Ron Hubbard's Saint Hill laboratory at the midpoint of the twentieth century is just as verdant today. Moreover, when further considering what LRH discoveries signaled vis-à-vis plants as sentient organisms responding to communication and affinity in ways paralleling all other living things, we indeed come to worldview. While even more than that, we come to whole new vistas of possibilities wherein Mankind may embrace the plant kingdom and so become that much more alive. ■

The Secret Life of Plants: yet another derivative offshoot from original LRH research and a New Age touchstone as of 1972. Also taking root in the cultural bedrock was a Stevie Wonder soundtrack to the documentary film.

Closing Note

"Some discoveries of considerable

interest to horticulture have

been made at Saint Hill."

—*L. Ron Hubbard*

As we have seen, those discoveries were also of considerable interest well beyond the bounds of horticulture and a new worldview has indeed taken root. Yet lest one imagines this story is over, we offer one more word of perspective: for all that came to light in L. Ron Hubbard's Saint Hill greenhouse, his horticultural experimentation consumed but six partial months. Moreover, that experimentation represents but a circumstantial study of his greater life's work. To be sure, we have only touched the barest tip of profound revelations and readers are now invited to consider what else L. Ron Hubbard provided in the name of survival for all.

APPENDIX

Glossary | 121
Index | 151

GLOSSARY

𝒜

acidify: make (soil) acid. Most plants grow better in soil that is neutral, as opposed to soil that is acid. By *acid* is meant any of a large class of sour-tasting, corrosive substances. There are many different acids of varying strengths, from weak (such as lemon juice and vinegar) to strong (such as the acid in a car battery). Page 54.

acre, (upper one): an *acre* is a unit of land area equal to 4,840 square yards (0.405 hectare). Hence *upper one acre,* an acre situated at a higher level or farther north. Page 23.

affinity: a natural liking for or attraction to a person, thing, idea, etc. Page 115.

agrotechnical: of or having to do with *agrotechnology,* the technology of agriculture, which involves the methods, machinery, etc., needed for efficient agricultural production. Page 12.

Airdrie: a city in south central Scotland, 11 miles (18 kilometers) east of Glasgow. Page 94.

akin: having a similar quality or character. Page 86.

albeit: although; even if. Page 7.

alchemical: of or using a magical power or process to change something with relatively little value into something valuable. Likened to using *alchemy,* a type of chemistry, especially from about 1100 to 1500, that dealt with trying to find a way to change ordinary metals into gold and with trying to find a medicine that would cure any disease. Page 32.

almond skin: a firm, woody covering over the white, inner part of the almond. Almonds can be treated with hot water to soften the skin, enabling it to be removed. Page 75.

ammonium sulphate: also *ammonium sulfate,* a white, crystalline, solid chemical compound used chiefly as a fertilizer. Page 42.

amputate: cut off (something), likened to cutting off a part of the body. Page 21.

anthropomorphic: represented with human characteristics or with a human form. Page 98.

aphis (aphides): *aphis,* singular, *aphides* (or *aphids*), plural, any of numerous tiny, soft-bodied insects of worldwide distribution that suck the sap from the stems and leaves of various plants. Page 72.

apocryphal: believed to be true, though possibly not proven as factual. Page 12.

arboreal: of or about trees. Page 78.

atomic and molecular theory: the subject or study of the structure and energy of *atoms* and *molecules* and the relationship between them. An *atom* is a very small particle that is considered the building block of physical matter. All the material on Earth is composed of various combinations of atoms that unite in an infinite number of ways into more complex structures called molecules. A *molecule* is one of the basic units of matter, consisting of one or more atoms held together by chemical forces. Page 9.

Atomic Gardening Society: a group founded in the United Kingdom in the mid-twentieth century that promoted the use of radiation in gardening for the improvement of plants. Page 10.

axiomatic: based on or having to do with *axioms,* statements of natural laws on the order of those of the physical sciences. Page 85.

azalea: a flowering shrub that is widely grown for its large pink, purple, white, yellow or orange flowers. Page 26.

B

backwater: a place or situation regarded as cut off from the mainstream of activity or development and consequently seen as quiet or uneventful. From the literal meaning of *backwater,* a small, still body of water connected to a river but not affected by its current. Page 94.

ball-cock: a device for regulating the supply of water in a tank or similar container. It consists essentially of a hollow, floating ball that is fixed to a rod. The rod is connected to a valve. As the ball rises or falls with the level of the water in the tank, it causes the valve to open or shut. This turns on the water to fill the tank and then turns it off when it has reached the specified level. Page 47.

bankrupt: bring about the financial ruin of; make so poor as to be unable to pay one's debts. Page 91.

barnyard fertilizer(s): fertilizer made with animal manure and often containing barnyard bedding materials, such as straw and wood chips. Page 90.

basic slag: *slag* is a substance produced during the process of making steel. In this process, chemicals are mixed with the hot, melted metal to remove impurities from the metal. Slag is the substance that is left over. The word *basic* in *basic slag* means that the chemicals used in this process are *bases,* substances that are opposite in effect to acids. The leftover basic slag is high in minerals that plants need, so it is often ground into small particles for use as a fertilizer. Page 74.

bay, at: arrested, cornered or impeded as in development or forward course or progress. Page 73.

BBC: short for *British Broadcasting Corporation,* a British radio and television broadcasting company. Page 1.

bearing fruit: producing *fruit,* any of the edible parts of plants, especially when fleshy and containing seeds. Page 1.

Bearwood: a district within the town of Smethwick, England. *See also* **Smethwick.** Page 76.

bedding plant: an ornamental plant that is suitable for planting with other plants in a flower bed to achieve a desired visual effect, usually for one season's display. Page 16.

bedrock: the fundamental principles forming a firm foundation on which something is based. From the unbroken, solid rock that underlies the soil on the surface of the Earth. Page 115.

beds: areas of soil prepared for plants or flowers, or areas where particular plants or flowers are growing. Page 3.

beet: also *beetroot,* a vegetable that is an edible root, round or pointed in shape and dark red or white in color. Beets are usually eaten cooked. Page 25.

begonia, (tuberous-rooted): a *begonia,* a widely grown houseplant and garden plant with ragged-edged leaves and brightly colored flowers, that is grown from a *tuber,* a fleshy, swollen part of a root. Tuberous-rooted begonias are one of the basic types of begonias, other types having roots that are not tuberous. Page 66.

bench glasshouse: same as a *potting house* or *pothouse. See* **potting house.** Page 25.

benchmark: pertaining to or used as a standard of excellence, achievement, etc., against which anything similar must be measured or judged. Page 24.

Bentley early flowering fert.: a fertiliser (also spelled *fertilizer*), in full, Bentley's Early-Flowering Chrysanthemum Fertiliser. The product was made by the Joseph Bentley Company, a firm located near Hull, in the northeastern part of England, that began in the late 1800s and has specialized in gardening supplies and equipment. Page 74.

bereft: deprived of something valued. Page 89.

black spot: a plant disease that causes black patches to form on leaves, particularly on roses. Page 76.

black stem rot: a plant disease caused by a type of fungus that causes the plant stem to become water soaked and discolored, finally collapsing. In tuberous-rooted begonias, this disease also attacks the tubers. *See also* **tuberous-rooted begonia.** Page 66.

blight: any of several plant diseases that can cause either wilting or death of the plant or of an affected part of the plant. Page 91.

bloom(s): the flower of a plant. Page 47.

bolt from the blue: something sudden and unexpected. Page 1.

bombarding: subjecting (a body or substance) to the impact of rapidly moving particles or radiation. Page 101.

bone meal: animal bones ground to a coarse powder, used as a fertilizer or in animal feed. Page 74.

bowl fire(s): a type of electric heater used during the mid-twentieth century, consisting of a metallic, bowl-shaped reflector surrounding a central heating element. Page 48.

box(es): a shallow, wooden, open-topped, rectangular frame used for holding and cultivating plants in greenhouses. Page 14.

breaking: (of news) suddenly becoming public. Page 60.

break of colour: also *color break,* an instance of a flower's color being modified so that the solid color normal to the petals is streaked with darker or lighter colors. Color breaks are usually due to an infection from a virus that attacks the plant. Page 72.

breeding: the development of new types of plants with improved characteristics. Page 32.

breeding ground: a place where many insects or animals of a specified kind live and produce their young. Page 72.

British Commonwealth: an association of countries, including England, Wales, Scotland, Northern Ireland and various self-governing states (such as Canada, Australia, New Zealand) that were formerly part of the British Empire. The Commonwealth was formally established in 1931 to encourage trade and friendly relations. Page 7.

brown spot(s): any of various plant diseases that produce brown discolorations on the leaves. Page 76.

Bryn: the name of a residence in Forest Row. *See also* **Forest Row.** Page 68.

bush vegetables: vegetables that grow on bushes, such as *beans* and *peas,* vegetables with edible seeds that grow in *pods,* long, narrow, flat parts of plants that contain the seeds and usually have a thick skin. Page 25.

C

called in: asked (for something that one owes, such as a debt) to be repaid. Page 91.

cap: provide a fitting climax or conclusion to. Page 22.

capacity: 1. actual or potential ability to perform or do something. Page 38.
2. a specified role or position. Page 60.

catalyst: a person who acts as the stimulus in bringing about a change or result. Page 113.

catalyze: increase the rate or amount of activity or action (of something). Page 18.

categorically: absolutely, certainly and unconditionally, with no room for doubt, question or contradiction. Page 87.

Cedar of Lebanon: a type of cedar tree with horizontally spreading branches. Native to Lebanon and Turkey, such trees have a long life span and may reach 100 feet (30 meters) in height. Page 78.

cellular: having to do with a *cell,* the smallest structural unit of an organism that is capable of independent functioning. All plants and animals are made up of one or more cells that usually combine to form various tissues. Page 107.

Central Intelligence Agency: a United States Government agency created in 1947. The stated purpose of the CIA is to gather information (intelligence) and conduct secret operations to protect the country's national security. Page 113.

check: prevent something from increasing or continuing, as in *"check and prevent the spread of mildew."* Page 38.

cherry tomato: a variety of tomato having cherry-sized, edible, red or yellow fruit. Page 25.

chill: a cold atmospheric condition. Page 14.

China, prerevolutionary: a reference to China in the period from roughly 1928 until 1949. During this time the government was controlled by the Chinese *Nationalists,* the political party that had overturned the emperor (1911) and established China as a nation with elected leaders. After 1928, the Nationalists tried to block a revolution by the increasingly powerful Chinese Communists. A civil war eventually broke out. By 1949, with a Communist victory assured, the Nationalists moved to Taiwan, an island off the southeast coast of China, and set up a separate government. Page 9.

chrysanthemum: also *chrysanth,* a plant with brightly colored globe-shaped flowers with small densely clustered petals. From a Greek word meaning *gold flower,* from the color of one type of chrysanthemum. Page 25.

circa: used before a date to indicate that it is approximate or estimated; approximately. Page 9.

circumstantial: pertinent, but not of primary importance; accompanying or attending. Page 117.

cistern: a tank or container for storing or holding water. Page 47.

civics: the study of the principles and structure of government (in its relationship to citizens). Page 106.

cloche: a piece of clear material, sometimes on a frame, used to cover plants for a short time, usually to protect them from cold weather or to help them grow faster. Page 76.

cloud-capped: covered with clouds, as if with a cap; characterized by the presence of clouds; cloudy. Page 22.

cob(s): the hard core to which individual grains of corn are attached. Page 63.

cognitive: of or pertaining to the mental processes of perception, memory, judgment and reasoning. Page 113.

cold frame(s): a shallow, boxlike structure, usually made of wood or concrete, covered with glass or transparent plastic and used to protect plants (especially seedlings and small plants) from wind and cold temperatures without the use of artificial heat. Page 17.

commercial: 1. describes a product that can be bought by or is intended to be bought by the general public. Page 20.

2. relating to the buying and selling of goods or services as a business activity. Page 33.

Commonwealth, British: an association of countries, including England, Wales, Scotland, Northern Ireland and various self-governing states (such as Canada, Australia, New Zealand) that were formerly part of the British Empire. The Commonwealth was formally established in 1931 to encourage trade and friendly relations. Page 7.

compartmentalization: the action or state of dividing or being divided into separate areas, categories or sections. Page 102.

compost: 1. a mixture of several substances that help plants grow. Compost is particularly used for young plants and for those grown in pots. Page 54.

2. a mixture of decayed plants and other organic matter used by gardeners as a fertilizer for the soil. Page 61.

concerted: characterized as working hard to achieve something; determined. Page 54.

congenial: pleasant and friendly. Page 89.

constituent(s): a thing that, along with others, serves in making up a complete whole or unit; an essential part or component. Page 114.

contention: a state of angry disagreement and disharmony between people. Page 36.

cooped up: kept in a small, confined space. Page 94.

copiously: in large quantities or amounts; abundantly. Page 14.

cornstalk(s): the *stalk,* main stem, of a corn plant. Page 3.

cornucopia: figuratively, an abundant supply of good things. Literally, a *cornucopia,* or *horn of plenty,* is an ornament or container shaped like an animal's horn and overflowing with flowers, fruit and vegetables. Page 22.

corollary: that follows from or derives naturally from a circumstance or phenomenon; resulting. Page 86.

correlative: closely connected; mutually related; complementing one another. Page 3.

corroborated: confirmed or supported by evidence provided; made certain. Page 54.

Coventry: an industrial city in central England, located approximately 95 miles (153 kilometers) northwest of London. Coventry is known for the production of motor vehicles and aircraft engines. Traditionally part of the county of Warwickshire, Coventry became part of West Midlands in the mid-1970s. Page 66.

crabby: bad-tempered or irritable. Page 21.

creosote: a yellow or colorless oily substance having a strong smell, used as an *antiseptic,* a chemical that prevents infection by killing bacteria. Page 73.

crystalline: made of or resembling *crystals,* solid substances with an internal pattern of atoms that is regular, repeated and geometrically arranged. Hence *crystalline form,* a structure of a substance that is made of small particles that are, or are like, crystals. Page 18.

cucumber type house: a greenhouse in which to grow cucumbers, which need high temperature and humidity. This type of greenhouse is generally a building with a lower roof than other greenhouses, thus retaining the heat and humidity more easily. Page 67.

cultivated: loosened or broke up the ground. Page 23.

cultivation: the preparation and use of land for growing plants or crops. Page 1.

cutting compost: a mixture of several substances for growing *cuttings,* parts of stems or leaves that are cut off for rooting and becoming separate plants. *Cutting compost* is made up of substances that will supply the plant with the necessary nutrients and that will also permit good drainage, since cuttings are liable to rot if allowed to sit in too much moisture. Page 66.

cutting(s): a piece cut from a stem or leaf of a plant and capable of growing into a new plant. Page 18.

cutworm: a caterpillar that feeds at night on the stems and roots of young plants, often cutting them off near the surface of the ground. Cutworms hide in soil during the day. Page 74.

cycle-of-action: the sequence that an action goes through, wherein the action is started, is continued for as long as is required and then is completed as planned; start, change and stop. Page 103.

cyclical: of or pertaining to a cycle or cycles, or characterized by recurrence in cycles. A *cycle* is a period of time during which a characteristic, a regularly repeated event or a sequence of events occurs. Page 9.

D

Daily Mirror: a daily morning newspaper published in London and having one of the largest circulations of any newspaper in the country. Founded in 1903, it covers British culture, politics, economics, business, foreign affairs, sports and fashion. Page 94.

DDT: a powerful insecticide used especially against disease-carrying and crop-eating insects. *DDT* is an abbreviation for the longer chemical name of the substance. Page 93.

derivative: using or taken from other sources; not original. Page 1.

Dianetics: Dianetics is a forerunner and substudy of Scientology. Dianetics means "through the mind" or "through the soul" (from Greek *dia,* through, and *nous,* mind or soul). Dianetics is further defined as what the mind or soul is doing to the body. Page 7.

disposition: one's normal frame of mind, nature or characteristic attitude. Page 21.

dissected: examined minutely, part by part; analyzed. Page 22.

diversify: produce a variety of different types of crops, products, etc. Page 7.

downs: treeless, hilly areas with fairly smooth slopes usually covered with grass, particularly as found in southern England. Page 12.

Dracaena massangeana: a type of tropical shrub or tree with wide, sword-shaped leaves, popular as a houseplant. Also known as the *corn plant* or *fragrant Dracaena*. Page 113.

drew fire: figuratively, brought criticism. From the literal meanings of *draw,* bring on or attract, and *fire,* shooting. Page 113.

drill(s): a shallow furrow or trench into which seed is sown. Page 23.

drive(ing): provide momentum toward the successful operation or functioning of something. Page 18.

dubbed: gave a descriptive name to something; called. Page 22.

dwarf bean: any of various beans that form a comparatively small plant. Page 26.

dwarf pea: a type of pea that grows as a small, compact bush. Page 26.

dynamics: the dynamics are the urge to survive, expressed through a spectrum, with eight divisions. These are urges for survival as or through (1) self; (2) sex, the family and the future generation; (3) groups; (4) Mankind; (5) life, all organisms; (6) matter, energy, space and time—MEST—the physical universe; (7) spirits; and (8) the Supreme Being. Page 102.

E

early(ies): a plant that flowers relatively soon in the year. Specifically, a chrysanthemum classified as *early,* or *early-flowering,* refers to a variety that can be planted outdoors in spring and that will bloom from late summer to early autumn. *See also* **late(s).** Page 72.

East Grinstead: a town in West Sussex, England, approximately 30 miles (48 kilometers) south of London. Sussex is a former county of southeastern England, now divided into East Sussex and West Sussex. Page 1.

East Grinstead Courier: a newspaper in East Grinstead, West Sussex, England, primarily covering local news, business and community events. Page 7.

effected: brought about; produced as a result; caused. Page 32.

electrode(s): either of two points by which an electric current enters or leaves a battery or other electrical device. The electrodes connected to the E-Meter are the size of and shaped like cans and are held in the hands. Page 85.

electromagnetic spectrum: the range (spectrum) of *electromagnetic waves,* waves of energy made up of electric and magnetic fields traveling together. This range goes from long to short wavelengths. *Wavelength* is the distance from peak to peak in a wave. The longest electromagnetic waves are radio waves. Shorter waves include *infrared,* invisible radiation just below the red portion of visible light. Then visible light itself, which includes all the colors. Still shorter are the waves of *ultraviolet,* invisible radiation just above the blue portion of visible light. Then X-rays and, shortest of all, nuclear radiation. *See also* **infrared; light spectrum analysis; ultraviolet; X-ray(s).** Page 36.

Electropsychometer: the full name of the *E-Meter,* from electro (electricity), psyche (soul) and meter (measure); an electronic device for measuring the mental state or change of state of Homo sapiens. It is not a lie detector. It does not diagnose or cure anything. It is used by auditors to assist a person in locating areas of spiritual distress or travail. Page 85.

elemental: fundamental; basic and essential. Page 1.

E-Meter: full name *Electropsychometer,* from electro (electricity), psyche (soul) and meter (measure); an electronic device for measuring the mental state or change of state of Homo sapiens. It is not a lie detector. It does not diagnose or cure anything. It is used by auditors to assist a person in locating areas of spiritual distress or travail. Page 85.

emulsion, paraffin: a liquid used as an insecticide. *Paraffin* (British term for *kerosene*) is a clear liquid with a strong smell, made from coal or petroleum and used as a fuel in heaters and lights. It is stirred vigorously into a liquid soap that has been mixed with hot water. The paraffin and soapy water form an *emulsion,* a mixture that results when one liquid is added to another but does not dissolve into it. Paraffin emulsion, diluted and sprayed on plants, is a traditional method of controlling harmful insects. Page 73.

engender: bring into existence; produce. Page 114.

ensconced: settled or established in a comfortable place. Page 1.

ES lampholders: *lampholders* are the sockets into which a light bulb (lamp) fits and makes electrical contact when screwed in. *ES* stands for *Edison screw,* the base of a light bulb that has a raised line (thread) around it. The thread allows the light bulb to be fixed in place in the socket by twisting. The Edison screw was developed in 1909 by American inventor Thomas Edison (1847–1931). Page 40.

Esq.: an abbreviation for *esquire,* a chiefly British term appended to a man's name as a polite title when no other title is used, especially in a letter. Page 67.

Evening Citizen: a newspaper published in Glasgow, Scotland, from 1877 to 1974 and the first of the city's three evening newspapers. Glasgow is located in the southwestern part of Scotland and is the largest city in the country. Page 94.

ever-bearing: always producing something. *Ever* means at any time and *bearing* means yielding something by a natural process or producing something desirable or valuable. Page 38.

exacerbated: made worse, said of an already bad or problematic situation. Page 9.

expedient: suitable, practical or efficient in achieving a particular end; fit, proper or advantageous under the circumstances. Page 36.

extraction fan: a fan used to remove air, steam, smoke or unpleasant smells from a room or building. Page 49.

F: an abbreviation for *Fahrenheit. See also* **Fahrenheit.** Page 18.

Fahrenheit: a temperature scale on which water freezes at 32 degrees and boils at 212 degrees under normal atmospheric conditions. For example, a Fahrenheit temperature of 70 degrees is approximately 21.5 degrees *Celsius,* the temperature scale on which water freezes at 0 degrees and boils at 100 degrees. Page 49.

fallout: airborne radioactive dust and material shot into the atmosphere by a nuclear explosion, which then settles to the ground. *Radioactive* describes a substance that sends out harmful energy in the form of streams of very small particles from the decay (breaking down) of atoms within the substance. Page 9.

fancy: of particular excellence; of a quality distinctly above the average; specially selected. Used especially of food and, in some systems of grading, designating the highest of a series of grades of quality. Page 91.

feature: 1. a special article in a newspaper or magazine, often prominently displayed, that deals with a particular subject. Page 32.
2. include as an important part. Page 46.
3. a distinct or outstanding quality. Page 64.

fertilization: the improvement of the quality of soil, as for the production of crops. Page 1.

fertilizers: substances usually added to or spread onto soil to increase its ability to support plant growth. Fertilizers include organic materials, such as manure, and important chemical nutrients. Page 9.

fibrous: containing, consisting of or resembling *fibers,* fine threadlike pieces of plants. Page 61.

fleeting: fading or vanishing; dying out. Page 22.

flower show: an event or competition involving the public display of flowers, plants, garden design and the like. Page 86.

fluorescent (bulb): a reference to an electric lamp that consists of a glass bulb coated on the inside and containing a gas. An electric current passes through the gas, causing it to give off a form of light that is not visible. When this light strikes the coating on the inside of the tube, the coating begins to fluoresce (glow) with visible light. Page 36.

fodder: coarse food for cattle, horses, etc., composed of leaves, stalks and grain of such plants as corn. Page 23.

foliage: the leaves of a plant or tree. Page 37.

foliated: covered with leaves. Page 8.

"food of the gods": food that is worthy of being consumed by gods, as in Greek mythology, where only gods could eat certain food, as it gave them eternal life. Page 3.

forcing: of or concerning speeding up the development or maturity of (plants, fruit, etc.), as by the use of heat, special lighting or the like. Page 108.

foremost: first, before any other or anything else in position, rank or importance. Page 66.

Forest Row: a town in southern England, about 30 miles (48 kilometers) from London. Forest Row is located at the edge of the *Ashdown Forest,* a partly wooded area of countryside that historically was a royal hunting park. Page 68.

freak: oddly different from what is usual or normal. Page 33.

free-form: not carefully planned or organized; encouraged to evolve without advance planning. Page 12.

frequency(ies): the measurement of the number of lightwaves that pass by a certain point in space in a given amount of time, usually measured in number of cycles, or vibrations, per second. For example, visible light can be divided into a series of colors, in the order violet, blue, green, yellow, orange and red. Each color has a different frequency, red being the lowest, then progressing through the colors to violet (at the opposite end) being the highest. Page 3.

fruit, bearing: producing *fruit,* any of the edible parts of plants, especially when fleshy and containing seeds. Page 1.

fruition: a state or point in which something has come to maturity or had a desired outcome. Page 20.

fungus: plural *fungi,* organisms that live by decomposing and absorbing the organic material (such as plants) in which they grow. Page 38.

G

galvanic: relating to or produced by a current of electricity, especially one produced by chemical action. In a plant, electrical currents can pass from one part of the plant to another by means of chemical action, similar to the way the nerves in a body transmit electrical currents. In the case of plants, they have cells that transmit electricity by means of increases and decreases in the levels of certain chemicals. This can cause the plant to have a *"galvanic shock"* when injured. Page 89.

galvanometer: an instrument for detecting and measuring small electrical currents. Page 100.

Garden News: one of Britain's most popular gardening newspapers. Published weekly, it provides the latest gardening news, practical advice and tips. Page 32.

gaseous: giving off gases. Materials that are used as mulch for plants, such as compost, give off various gases as they decompose and undergo chemical changes. Page 17.

George Washington University: a private university, founded in 1821, in the city of Washington, DC. Named after the first president of the United States, George Washington (1732–1799), it maintains various schools of education, including the School of Engineering and Applied Science and the Columbian College of Arts and Sciences. The university has a long history of supporting research in physics and other technical fields. Page 9.

geranium(s): a popular garden plant with large rounded leaves and bright red, pink or white flowers on tall stalks. Page 10.

germination: the action of a seed starting to grow into a plant. Page 16.

glade(s): an open space in a wood or forest. Page 9.

Glasgow: a seaport and the largest city in Scotland, located in the southwestern part of the country. Glasgow has traditionally been a center of shipbuilding, manufacturing and commerce. Page 94.

glasshouse: a chiefly British term for a *greenhouse*. *See also* **greenhouse.** Page 8.

Golden Cross Bantam (Hybrid): a type of sweet corn developed in the early 1930s as a variety that would withstand a disease that severely affected sweet corn. A *hybrid* is a plant produced from a cross between two plants that differ slightly in their genetic makeup. Page 23.

Golden Hummer corn: a type of American sweet corn. *Hummer* is a slang term meaning excellent. Page 23.

grave: threatening a seriously bad outcome or involving serious issues; critical. Page 18.

greenhouse: a building, room or area, usually chiefly of glass, in which the temperature is maintained within a desired range, used for cultivating delicate plants or growing plants out of season. Page 1.

green thumb(s): an exceptional aptitude for gardening or for growing plants successfully. Also called *green fingers*. Page 12.

grotto: a structure in a garden built to resemble a cool, attractive cave, surrounded with trees and other plants and often incorporating a fountain, pool of water or the like. Page 22.

grow lights: lamps giving out electric light that plants can use to grow indoors. Page 3.

guinea pig: someone who agrees to be the subject of a test or trial. Literally, a *guinea pig* is a plump, short-eared, furry domesticated animal, native to South America, widely kept as a pet and used as a subject in scientific experiments. Page 93.

H

Hamilton: a city in south central Scotland, 12 miles (19 kilometers) southeast of Glasgow. Page 94.

hardy: capable of surviving under less-than-favorable conditions; sturdy and healthy. Page 104.

heartening: making (one) feel happier and more positive. Page 104.

heavy-footed: clumsy, insensitive or overly forceful. Page 90.

heels of, on the: closely following; just after. Page 62.

Helena: city and capital of Montana, a state in the northwestern United States bordering on Canada. Page 7.

heredity: the passing on of characteristics genetically from one generation to another. Page 89.

high-pressure: vigorously energetic and persistent in seeking to bring about a result. Page 14.

Hill, Amelia Leavitt: (?–1962) American decorative arts scholar and author who wrote numerous books on topics including gardening, flower arranging, antiques and home remodeling. Page 10.

hill(s): a small mound of soil formed over a seed or around a plant. Page 23.

hitherto: up to this time; until now. Page 101.

Holyoke Daily Transcript & Telegram: a daily newspaper published in Holyoke, a city in western Massachusetts (a state in the northeastern part of the United States). Originating as a weekly in 1846 and becoming a daily in 1882, the newspaper was the major publication for the Holyoke area. It closed in 1993. Page 114.

horticulture: the science and art of cultivating flowers, fruits, vegetables or ornamental plants. Page 1.

host: a very large number; a great quantity. Page 113.

hothouse: another name for a *greenhouse. See also* **greenhouse.** Page 7.

house(s): short for *glasshouse* or *greenhouse. See also* **greenhouse.** Page 13.

hthse: an abbreviation for *hothouse,* which is another name for a *greenhouse. See also* **greenhouse.** Page 30.

Hubbard Communications Office: the Office of L. Ron Hubbard, originally organized with the purpose of handling and expediting the communication lines of LRH. The Hubbard Communications Office was later made one of the divisions of every Scientology organization and was assigned responsibility for building, holding, maintaining and manning the organization. Page 61.

humidity: the amount of moisture in the air. Page 70.

humus: a general term for the soil in which plants grow. Page 65.

"hunt": swing back and forth. Page 93.

hydrangea: a shrub that bears white, pink or bluish flowers. Each small flower grows with many others in large, showy clusters. Page 26.

I

iconic: characteristic of an *icon,* something widely admired, especially when viewed as symbolizing a place, time period, culture or the like. Page 86.

Ideal Scene: a *scene* is an area, a place where an activity or event takes place. An *Ideal Scene* is the way an area ought to be. If one doesn't have an idea of how a real activity (such as a part of one's job, environment or life) should operate, then obvious departures from the Ideal Scene are not noticed. Page 107.

immersion heater: an electric heating element that is positioned in a liquid to be heated, typically in a water tank. Page 47.

infallible: something that is unfailing in effectiveness or is certain. Page 1.

infinitesimal: extremely small. Page 85.

infrared: a form of light considered invisible, having a wavelength just longer than that of red light. Red light has the longest wavelength of visible light detected by the human eye, which can see colors from violet (shortest wavelength) through blue, green, yellow, orange and red (longest wavelength). By using infrared, which has a penetrating heating effect on objects around it, the soil in the greenhouse is heated but not the air, thus eliminating the danger of mildew or fungus on the plants. Page 10.

inhospitable: harsh and difficult to live or work in. Page 7.

insentient: not conscious or capable of perceptions; not consciously perceiving. Page 92.

interwoven: connected closely; intermingled. Page 1.

intrinsically: in a manner that belongs to something as one of the basic and essential elements that make it what it is. Page 85.

irradiate: expose to radiation. *See also* **radiation** and **soft radiation.** Page 32.

irrespective of: without regard to; independent of. Page 36.

irrigation: the artificial watering of land (as by pipes, sprinklers, canals, ditches or flooding) to supply moisture for plant growth. Page 9.

J

Jaipur, Maharajah of: Sawai Man Singh II (1912–1970), the last ruler of Jaipur in India, before India became a republic in 1950, and owner of Saint Hill Manor during the 1950s. A *maharajah* is a former title used in India for a king or prince, especially the ruler of one of the larger regions. *Jaipur* is a former state in northwestern India, now part of the state of Rajasthan. It is also the name of the chief city of the region, now the capital of Rajasthan. Page 7.

juncture: a particular point in time or in the development of events. Page 87.

K

Kent: a county in southeastern England. Page 72.

kingdom, plant: one of the three broad divisions of natural objects: the animal, vegetable (plant) and mineral kingdoms. A *kingdom* is a region or sphere of nature. Page 1.

L

ladybird (ladybug): a small beetle with a rounded body, usually red or yellow with black spots. Because they feed chiefly on harmful insects and their eggs, these beetles are often purchased in quantities and released in gardens and greenhouses for pest control. Page 73.

lapse: a brief falling or slipping away, as from a standard; an error. Page 108.

larvae: plural of *larva,* a form of an insect that resembles a worm and that continues to grow until fully developed into an adult form, such as a beetle. Page 73.

late(s): a plant that flowers at an advanced season of the year. Specifically, a chrysanthemum classified as *late,* or *late-flowering,* refers to a variety grown in pots outdoors in summer, then brought into a greenhouse, where it will flower from autumn until late winter. *See also* **early(ies).** Page 72.

lavishes: gives a lot (of something). Page 14.

"lazybones": done by using as little energy as possible. Page 61.

leaf miner: any of the larvae of a type of small fly or moth that feeds by burrowing between the two surfaces of a leaf, causing damage to the leaf. *See also* **larvae.** Page 73.

leaf mold: a rich soil consisting chiefly of decayed leaves. The term *mold* here (also spelled *mould*) means loose, soft, easily worked soil, especially when rich with decayed animal or vegetable matter and good for growing plants. Page 54.

ledger book: a record book, normally consisting of pages with lined columns for entering numbers and other information. Page 31.

lest: in case that; in order to prevent any possibility that something will happen; for fear that. Page 117.

light spectrum analysis: the analysis of what color of light helps plants grow best, in reference to experiments conducted by L. Ron Hubbard at Saint Hill in 1959 in which plants were grown under several different colors of lights and their growth rate was recorded. *Spectrum* (also *light spectrum* or *color spectrum*) means the series of colors into which visible light can be divided: violet, blue, green, yellow, orange and red. Each color has a different wavelength, red being the longest, then progressing through the colors to violet (at the opposite end), the shortest. Page 10.

Lilliput: a pocket-sized magazine published in England during the mid-1900s, with stories, articles, photographs and illustrations. The name is from the fictional land of Lilliput, where the people and environment are only 1/12 the size of normal people and things, from the satiric work *Gulliver's Travels* (1726) by English author Jonathan Swift (1667–1745). Page 95.

loath: unwilling or reluctant (to do something). Page 72.

louvre: also spelled *louver,* a frame on a door or window supporting spaced horizontal slats angled to admit air and light but not rain. Page 49.

$\mathcal{M}$

Maharajah of Jaipur: Sawai Man Singh II (1912–1970), the last ruler of Jaipur in India, before India became a republic in 1950, and owner of Saint Hill Manor during the 1950s. A *maharajah* is a former title used in India for a king or prince, especially the ruler of one of the larger regions. *Jaipur* is a former state in northwestern India, now part of the state of Rajasthan. It is also the name of the chief city of the region, now the capital of Rajasthan. Page 7.

manure: animal waste matter, often mixed with straw, used as fertilizer for soil. Page 54.

Margate: a city and seaside resort located in the northeastern part of Kent, a county in southeastern England. Page 72.

market gardener: a person who tends a *market garden,* a plot of ground or small farm where fruit, vegetables and sometimes flowers are grown for sale rather than for the grower's own use. Page 12.

master(s): a man who is the owner of a house and the head of the family that lives there. Page 1.

maven: a person who is experienced and knowledgeable in some special field; an expert. Page 10.

maxim: a statement of a general rule or truth. Page 20.

Mazoe: a region in the southern African country of Zimbabwe (earlier Southern Rhodesia), near Harare (earlier Salisbury) and the location of one of the country's oldest agricultural estates. Page 70.

meandering: following an indirect route or course, especially one with a series of twists and turns. Page 12.

memo: a short form of *memorandum,* a written communication, similar to a letter, that is intended for a person or people who work in an office or organization. Page 12.

mercury vapor (light): a type of light produced when electricity is passed through a gas (vapor, also spelled *vapour*) that consists of mercury. (*Mercury* is a heavy silver-colored metal that is liquid at ordinary temperatures and is often used in thermometers.) Page 36.

meteoric: developing very fast and attracting a lot of attention. Page 7.

methodology: the methods or organizing principles underlying a particular art, science or other area of study. Page 10.

mildew: a plant disease in which the parasitic fungus is visible as white or gray powdery deposits on the leaves or fruit. Page 10.

mind-set: a set of beliefs or a way of thinking that determines a person's behavior and outlook; attitude or inclination. Page 1.

mineral(s): minute amounts of metallic elements naturally occurring in the earth that are vital for the healthy growth of plants and animals. Page 20.

min–max thermometer: a thermometer that can measure the minimum and maximum temperature during a day. Such thermometers are commonly used wherever a simple means is needed to measure the extremes of temperature in a given location. The thermometer consists of a U-shaped tube with two scales, one for the minimum temperature and one for the maximum. Each arm of the tube contains a small marker that stops at the highest and lowest point of the temperature scale. Page 49.

mold: a furry type of growth on the surface of animal or vegetable matter, especially in the presence of dampness or decay. Page 22.

mold, leaf: a rich soil consisting chiefly of decayed leaves. The term *mold* here (also spelled *mould*) means loose, soft, easily worked soil, especially when rich with decayed animal or vegetable matter and good for growing plants. Page 54.

moot: open to argument. Page 113.

Moscow Agricultural Academy: an institution of higher learning located in Moscow, Russia, and the oldest such school in Russia. Founded in 1865, the Moscow Agricultural Academy offers instruction and academic degrees in a number of fields, including horticulture, animal science, soil science and economics. Page 113.

Mother Nature: the protecting or controlling force of the natural world, regarded as a person. Page 22.

Motherwell: a city in south central Scotland, 13 miles (21 kilometers) southeast of Glasgow. Page 94.

MR: also *Mr.,* an abbreviation for *Mister,* the customary title of courtesy used with the name of a man. Page 66.

mulch: a mass of leaves, bark or other organic material spread around or over plants to prevent excessive evaporation or erosion, maintain even soil temperature, enrich the soil and inhibit weed growth. Page 17.

mutant: undergoing or resulting from mutation. *See also* **mutate.** Page 9.

mutate: bring about *mutation,* a random change in the hereditary material of an organism's cells, resulting in a new trait or characteristic, as distinguished from a variation resulting from generations of gradual change. Various influences can cause the hereditary material to change, including electronic particles, beams or rays striking the body. This change is then passed on to the organism's offspring. Page 3.

myriad: a great number of things. Page 92.

Natal Witness: a daily newspaper of South Africa, founded in 1846 and the oldest continuously published newspaper in the country. _Natal_ is a former province of eastern South Africa, merged in 1994 with KwaZulu to form the province of KwaZulu-Natal. The _Natal Witness_ is published in Pietermaritzburg, the capital city of KwaZulu-Natal. Page 114.

Naval School of Military Government: a school of military government established at Princeton University, Princeton, New Jersey, in October 1944. The purpose was to train navy officers so as to provide needed personnel for projected military government activities as well as for specialized civilian duties. Page 9.

nerve: bravery or confidence necessary to do something considered difficult, unpleasant or the like. Page 16.

New Age: of or relating to a social movement that began in the late twentieth century, which draws on ancient concepts, especially from Eastern and Native American traditions, and incorporates such ideas and practices as concern for nature, belief in reincarnation, astrology, meditation and vegetarianism. Page 113.

nitrate(s): a fertilizer that consists of various chemical compounds that include nitrogen. Nitrates contain nutrients that promote plant growth. Page 20.

Northwest: the northwestern part of the United States, including the states of Washington, Oregon, Idaho and Montana. Page 7.

nursery(ies): a place where plants and trees are grown, especially for sale. Page 62.

oatmeal: a soft food made by boiling grains (specifically oats) in milk or water until thick. A North American term for _porridge._ Page 21.

offshoot: something that originated or developed from something else. Page 115.

order of life: a class, kind or type of living thing. Page 3.

organic: affecting, relating to or derived from a plant or animal. Page 88.

Orthocide: the brand name of a _fungicide,_ a type of chemical treatment for killing _fungus,_ an organism that lives by decomposing and absorbing the organic material (such as plants) in which they grow. _Orthocide_ is a fungicide designed to eliminate plant diseases, such as stem rot, that are caused by a fungus. _See also_ **black stem rot.** Page 66.

Ottawa Citizen: a daily newspaper founded in 1845 and the largest newspaper in _Ottawa,_ capital of Canada, located in the southeastern part of the country. The logo of the newspaper features the summit of the _Peace Tower,_ a Canadian landmark, located in Ottawa. Page 114.

outgrowth: a development or result, likened to something that grows directly out from something else, such as a main part. Page 113.

overdraft: the amount that an account holder owes a bank because the balance in the account does not cover the amount that he or she has withdrawn from it. Page 91.

𝒫

Paleozoic: noting or pertaining to an era occurring between 570 million and 230 million years ago, characterized by the first appearance of fish, insects, reptiles and seed-bearing plants. Page 87.

paper rings: rings about 2 or 3 inches (51 or 76 millimeters) tall, formed of stiff paper or cardboard and used in gardens to protect young plants from cutworms. The ring is placed over the plant and pushed down into the soil to a depth of about ½ inch (13 millimeters) so that cutworms cannot attack and eat the stem of the plant. *See also* **cutworm.** Page 75.

paper(s): 1. an essay or article, such as one that is prepared for publication on an academic subject. Page 9.

2. a printed publication, typically issued daily or weekly, consisting of folded unstapled sheets and containing news, articles and advertisements. Page 62.

paraffin emulsion: a liquid used as an insecticide. *Paraffin* (British term for *kerosene*) is a clear liquid with a strong smell, made from coal or petroleum and used as a fuel in heaters and lights. It is stirred vigorously into a liquid soap that has been mixed with hot water. The paraffin and soapy water form an *emulsion,* a mixture that results when one liquid is added to another but does not dissolve into it. Paraffin emulsion, diluted and sprayed on plants, is a traditional method of controlling harmful insects. Page 73.

parasite: an organism that lives on or in another organism, known as the *host,* from the body of which it obtains its food. Page 107.

Parliament: a reference to the national legislative (lawmaking) body of Great Britain, made up of two groups, one consisting of elected representatives (House of Commons) and the other, members of the nobility and high-ranking clergy (House of Lords). Page 9.

pastoral: of or relating to the countryside as contrasted with the city; rural. Page 7.

P.B.: an abbreviation for *post box,* a numbered box in a post office assigned to a person or organization, where letters for them are kept until called for. Page 70.

pearl bulb: an electric light bulb that is frosted on the inside so as to diffuse the light. *See also* **pearl white.** Page 43.

pearl white: a pale grayish-white color tinged with blue. Page 43.

peat moss: *moss* is a nonflowering plant with short stems and small leaves that grows in moist, shady areas. *Peat moss* is any of these plants that form *peat,* a material found in marshy or damp regions, composed of partially decayed plants. Once dried, peat moss is used chiefly as a mulch or to prepare ground for seeding. Page 17.

perennial: regularly repeated or continuing. Page 60.

perpendiculars, rule giving two: a type of ruler (rule) for drawing and measuring, consisting of sections that are perpendicular (at an angle of 90 degrees). Page 29.

perpetual: continuing indefinitely without interruption; unceasing; constant. Page 24.

phosphate(s): a fertilizing material containing compounds of *phosphorus,* a chemical element important to plant growth. Page 20.

photosynthesis: the process by which green plants and certain other organisms use the energy of light to convert carbon dioxide and water into food. Page 36.

pink(s): a plant with sweet-smelling pink or white flowers and slender gray-green leaves. Page 76.

pivotal: of vital or critical importance. Page 86.

plant kingdom: one of the three broad divisions of natural objects: the animal, vegetable (plant) and mineral kingdoms. A *kingdom* is a region or sphere of nature. Page 1.

plot(s): a small area of ground, especially an area devoted to a particular purpose, such as growing flowers or vegetables. Page 23.

pole-bean(s): a climbing green bean that is trained to grow upright and is supported on a pole, fence, etc. Page 93.

polythene: also called *polyethylene,* a tough, light, flexible plastic used for bags, packaging, etc. Page 79.

populace: all the inhabitants of a place; population. Page 22.

port(s): also called an *air port,* an opening to release or admit air. Page 14.

postulated: assumed to be true, real or necessary, especially as a basis for reasoning. Page 85.

potash: any of several potassium compounds, often occurring naturally and used especially in industry and as fertilizers in agriculture. Potash was originally obtained by evaporating a solution containing wood ashes in iron pots, hence its name. Page 42.

pothouse: same as a *potting house. See* **potting house.** Page 25.

potting house: also *pothouse* or *bench glasshouse,* a type of greenhouse with benches on which to set pots of plants and where the plants can remain while they are growing. Page 14.

potty: a chiefly British term meaning foolish or crazy. Page 114.

predicated: based (on a given fact or facts). Page 102.

prerevolutionary China: a reference to China in the period from roughly 1928 until 1949. During this time the government was controlled by the Chinese *Nationalists,* the political party that had overturned the emperor (1911) and established China as a nation with elected leaders. After 1928, the Nationalists tried to block a revolution by the increasingly powerful Chinese Communists. A civil war eventually broke out. By 1949, with a Communist victory assured, the Nationalists moved to Taiwan, an island off the southeast coast of China, and set up a separate government. Page 9.

Press Agent: same as *press officer, press secretary* or the like. *See also* **Press Officer.** Page 102.

Press Officer: also *press agent, press secretary* or the like, a person officially in charge of establishing and maintaining relations with the press (newspapers, magazines, etc.) by supplying information, photographs and stories. Page 61.

presumption: an instance or example of behavior regarded as rude or inconsiderate. Page 66.

Princeton (University): a leading United States university located in Princeton, New Jersey (a state in the eastern United States). In the 1940s, it housed a school of government to train navy and army officers so as to provide needed personnel for projected military government activities. Page 9.

prodigious: extraordinary in size, amount, extent or degree. Page 1.

produce: products of farms or gardens, especially fruits and vegetables. Page 7.

profusion: a great quantity or amount. Page 12.

proliferated: spread and grew larger. Page 113.

prophesies: predicts what is going to happen in the future. Page 33.

propitious: presenting favorable conditions or indicating a favorable outcome. Page 7.

protocol: the plan for carrying out a scientific study. Page 22.

pruned: having had the excessive branches (of a plant) cut off, as for better growth. Page 12.

Q

qualms: uneasy feelings of doubt or conscience about an action or conduct. Page 21.

queer: strange or odd; not quite right; unusually different. Page 91.

quest: a search or pursuit made in order to find or obtain something. Page 54.

R

radiation: energy that is emanating (flowing or coming out from a source) in the form of either waves or particles and that can influence matter across space. Radiation includes such things as heat, light and X-rays, all of which have a relatively low energy level. Extremely high energy comes from atomic reactions and can, in large amounts, be harmful to living things. *See also* **soft radiation** and **X-ray(s).** Page 3.

radish: a small, red or white vegetable that is the root of the radish plant and is usually round or finger-shaped. Radishes are crisp and have a sharp taste. They are eaten raw in salads. Page 25.

reactive: characterized by *reaction,* happening in (immediate) response to an influence; responding to an influence in a particular way or with particular behavior; "stimulus-response" type behavior. From Latin *reagere,* to do or act back. Page 91.

reader: a book of collected or assorted writings, especially when related in authorship, theme or instructive purpose. Page 113.

regimen: a specific system, program, plan or course of action to attain some result. Page 12.

regimented: organized into a definite or uniform order or system. Page 106.

repercussion(s): an effect or result of some event or action, often one having a wide influence. Page 3.

replicate: do (something) again or copy (something); reproduce. Page 113.

resilient: able to withstand or recover quickly from difficult conditions. Page 32.

Reveille: a popular British weekly magazine that featured articles on lifestyle, fashion, music, gardening and sports, published between 1940 and 1979. The word *reveille* means a military wake-up signal played on a bugle. At its peak, the magazine's circulation numbered in the millions. Page 95.

reverence: respect for something as if sacred. Page 73.

Rhodesia, Southern: the former name of *Zimbabwe,* a country in Southern Africa. Page 70.

rhodie: a shortened form of *rhododendron,* a large evergreen bush with large flowers, usually bright pink, purple or white in color. Page 26.

ripple effect: a spreading effect or series of consequences caused by a single action or event. From the ripples that spread across the surface of a pool when something is dropped into the water. Page 113.

root crop: also called *root plants. See* **root plants.** Page 56.

root plants: plants grown for their large, edible roots, such as turnips, beets and potatoes. Page 25.

root system(s): the network of roots that a plant develops and spreads underground to anchor itself and to absorb water and nutrients from the soil. Page 90.

rotated crops: crops grown by *rotation,* a system in which the types of crops grown on the same piece of ground are varied so as to maintain soil fertility and prevent plant disease. Page 9.

rule giving two perpendiculars: a type of ruler (rule) for drawing and measuring, consisting of sections that are perpendicular (at an angle of 90 degrees). Page 29.

S

SAE Enclosed: in full, *self-addressed envelope enclosed,* a reference to having included an envelope with one's own name and address so that the recipient of one's letter can write back without having to supply his own envelope. Page 66.

Saint Hill: the name of the manor (large house and its land) purchased by L. Ron Hubbard in 1959, located in East Grinstead, Sussex, England. Saint Hill Manor served as LRH's home and was where he carried out much of his research from 1959 to 1966. Page 1.

sand: in classifications of types of soil, the type referred to as *sand* consists of a large proportion of actual grains of sand and smaller proportions of much finer material. Because the size of sand grains is fairly large, air and water (both of which are needed by plants) can move freely through such soil. Page 54.

sand, sharp: a coarse sand that has different-sized particles with sharp edges. Sharp sand has not been worn down and rounded by water, wind, etc. By comparison, sand with rounded particles is finer and is frequently found on beaches. Page 58.

saturation: a condition in which air at a specific temperature contains all the water vapor it can hold. Also, the state in which soil has been supplied with water until it reaches the point where no more can be absorbed. Page 14.

Scientology: the term Scientology is taken from the Latin *scio,* which means "knowing in the fullest sense of the word," and the Greek word *logos,* meaning "study of." In itself the word means literally "knowing how to know." Scientology is further defined as the study and handling of the spirit in relationship to itself, universes and other life. Page 3.

Scotch fir: also *Scotch pine,* a type of pine tree that has a reddish trunk and twisted, bluish-green needles. Page 26.

scrounged: found by looking or hunting around. Page 91.

seed box: a shallow box or tray in which seeds are placed and covered with a thin layer of soil so they can start to develop into seedlings. At the point when the seedlings are large enough to be handled, they are removed from the seed box and transplanted to continue growing. Page 14.

segregating: separating one thing from others or dividing things into separate groups kept apart from each other. Page 33.

sentient: conscious or capable of perceptions; consciously perceiving. Page 10.

"series of one on potatoes": a humorous reference to one experiment done on potatoes. Literally, a *series* is a group of three or more related things or events, one following another. Hence *"series of one on potatoes,"* an experiment performed on only the one item, potatoes, with no further similar tests done. Page 76.

serviceable: well suited for a purpose; effective. Page 49.

set: (of flowers) developed into fruit. Page 48.

70s.: an abbreviation for *70 shillings.* A *shilling* was a coin used in the United Kingdom prior to 1971, worth one-twentieth of a *pound,* the basic monetary unit of the UK. Page 44.

sharp sand: a coarse sand that has different-sized particles with sharp edges. Sharp sand has not been worn down and rounded by water, wind, etc. By comparison, sand with rounded particles is finer and is frequently found on beaches. Page 58.

shilling(s): a coin used in the United Kingdom prior to 1971, worth one-twentieth of a *pound,* the basic monetary unit of the UK. An abbreviation for *shilling* is *s.,* as in *70s.,* 70 shillings. Page 40.

shoot(s): a young branch, stem, twig or the like, often one that shoots off from some portion of a plant. Page 22.

Siemens: one of the leading electrical and electronics manufacturers in the world. Siemens was founded in Germany in the 1840s. Page 29.

Siemens type MAT/V Clear bulb: a designation for a type of electrical light bulb that produces light similar to daylight, manufactured by Siemens. *See also* **Siemens.** Page 29.

Siemens, type MBW/U 125 W: a designation for a type of electrical light bulb that produces ultraviolet light, manufactured by Siemens. *See also* **Siemens** and **ultraviolet.** Page 29.

sifted: examined thoroughly to isolate that which is important or useful. Page 10.

Smethwick: a town in central England situated on the outskirts of Birmingham (England's second-largest city and a major industrial center). Formerly in the county of Staffordshire (Staffs), Smethwick became part of the county of the West Midlands in 1974. Page 76.

sodium (lamp): an electric lamp containing neon gas and sodium vapor through which a current runs to produce an orange-yellow light used for street lighting. *Sodium* is a soft silver-white metallic element that reacts readily with other substances. *Neon* is a colorless, odorless gaseous element that occurs in very small quantities in the air and glows orange when electricity is passed through it. Page 36.

soft radiation: radiation that has relatively low energy and thus little penetrating power. Said of X-rays. *See also* **radiation** and **X-ray(s).** Page 3.

soil: the upper layer of earth in which plants grow, which is a mixture of mineral, plant and animal materials. There are many kinds of soils, each having certain characteristics, including color and composition. The kind of soil in an area helps determine how well crops grow there. The soil in some areas measures less than 5 inches (13 centimeters) deep. Other soils are more than 4 feet (1.2 meters) deep. Page 9.

Soil Association: an English environmental group founded in 1946 by farmers, scientists and nutritionists to promote beneficial farming practices and plant, animal and human health. Page 68.

soil chemistry: the chemical properties and reactions of different soils. Soil chemistry is affected by the amounts and types of mineral and organic substances found in soil. *See also* **soil.** Page 22.

sophisticated: involving or requiring systems, processes, equipment, machinery or the like that is complex or intricate. Page 113.

sophomore: a student in the second year of college in the United States. Page 9.

South American Popcorn: a variety of popcorn having large, yellow kernels that become distinctively mushroom shaped when popped. *Popcorn* is a type of corn whose kernels have a hard outer shell surrounding a soft, moist center. When the kernel is heated, its moisture turns to steam, causing the shell to burst. This turns the kernel inside out so that it forms a white, puffy mass. Page 26.

sow: scatter or plant seed in or on a field, ground, earth, etc., to grow crops. Page 22.

soya beans: also called *soybeans,* a widely cultivated farm crop originating in Asia and now a leading crop in the United States. Soya beans are used primarily to produce oil and protein-rich food and are also grown for soil improvement. Page 9.

specimen(s): an individual thing, such as a plant, used as an example or type for scientific study or examination. Page 76.

spectrum analysis, light: the analysis of what color of light helps plants grow best, in reference to experiments conducted by L. Ron Hubbard at Saint Hill in 1959 in which plants were grown under several different colors of lights and their growth rate was recorded. *Spectrum* (also *light spectrum* or *color spectrum*) means the series of colors into which visible light can be divided: violet, blue, green, yellow, orange and red. Each color has a different wavelength, red being the longest, then progressing through the colors to violet (at the opposite end), the shortest. Page 10.

springboard: anything serving as the starting point and providing the impetus (driving force) for an action or enterprise. (Literally, a *springboard* is a strong, flexible board from which a diver or gymnast may jump in order to gain added impetus.) Page 106.

sprinkler: a device that sends out a moving spray of water, used for watering lawns and gardens. Page 13.

spurring: encouraging or stimulating to greater activity. Page 62.

Staffs: an abbreviation for *Staffordshire,* a county in central England about 100 miles (160 kilometers) northwest of London. Its important industries include agriculture, dairy farming, the manufacture of porcelain and coal mining. Page 74.

staking: supporting a plant with a *stake,* a strong pole or stick with a pointed end that is pushed into the ground so the plant can climb along the pole as it grows. Page 48.

stalk plants: plants with a long stalk, main stem, such as corn. Page 25.

stock: 1. a type or group of plants. Page 34.
2. also *stalk,* the main stem of a plant, as distinguished from roots and smaller stems. Page 108.

strain(s): a distinct breed, stock or variety of an animal, plant or other organism. Page 22.

Strathaven: a town in south central Scotland, 23 miles (37 kilometers) southeast of Glasgow. Page 94.

string bean(s): any of various kinds of bean, as the green bean, whose pods (the long, narrow, outer cases holding the seeds of a plant) are cooked and eaten as vegetables. Page 18.

strip lighting: lighting consisting of long tubes (instead of bulbs) that provide illumination. Page 40.

stunt virus: a disease that causes plants to become *stunted,* prevented from reaching their normal growth. In chrysanthemums, a stunt virus results in smaller plants with flowers that are smaller and paler. Page 74.

substantially: to a great or significant extent; considerably. Page 49.

substantive: having practical importance, value or effect; real or actual; essential. Page 106.

sulphate of iron: also *sulfate of iron,* a substance occurring as light-green crystals and used as a weedkiller and disinfectant and in dyeing fabrics and making ink. It consists of the metal iron combined with *sulfur* (also *sulphur*), a pale-yellow element that exists in various physical forms, burns with a blue flame and a strong smell and is used in medicine and industry. Page 74.

summarily: promptly and without discussion; immediately. Page 113.

Sunday supplement(s): a separate section, especially a color magazine, added to the Sunday edition of a newspaper or periodical. Page 1.

sunny: exhibiting happiness; exceptionally cheerful and bright; optimistic. Page 21.

Sun, The: a daily newspaper in Melbourne, Australia, that ran from 1922 to 1990. During most of its history, *The Sun* had the highest circulation of any newspaper in the country. Melbourne is the second-largest city in Australia and is located in the southeastern part of the country. Page 114.

surplus(es): an amount or quantity in excess of what is needed; an amount left over when requirements have been met. Page 91.

Sussex: a former county of southeastern England, now divided into two counties, East Sussex and West Sussex. Saint Hill is located in East Grinstead, West Sussex. Page 1.

sustenance: nourishment that supports life; food. Page 18.

sweet corn: a variety of corn with kernels that contain a high concentration of sugar, eaten as a vegetable. Page 22.

sweet peas: climbing plants having large, fragrant flowers in blue, red, pink, purple and white. Page 37.

sylvan: full of woods or trees; pleasantly wooded and rural. Page 9.

synopsis: a brief or condensed statement giving a general view of something. Page 66.

synthesise: also *synthesize,* combine simple parts that unite with each other to make a new, more complex, whole. Page 114.

systemic: (of an insecticide) going through the entire system (the organism as a whole), specifically, entering a plant via the roots or shoots and passing through the tissues. In this way, plants become poisonous to insects that feed on them. Page 72.

$\mathcal{T}$

tap: a device by which a flow of liquid or gas from a pipe or container can be controlled; a faucet. Page 51.

tendril(s): literally, a thin, curling stem that grows from a climbing plant, used by the plant to attach itself to a wall or other support. Used figuratively for something that stretches out and attaches to other things. Page 113.

thermostat: a device that automatically regulates temperature or activates a device at a set temperature. Page 15.

***This Week* magazine:** the largest US Sunday supplement during the mid-1900s, carried by more than forty American newspapers. *This Week* was started in 1935 and at its peak in the early 1960s the magazine was distributed in more than fourteen million newspapers weekly. A *Sunday supplement* is a separate section, especially a color magazine, added to the Sunday edition of a newspaper or periodical. Page 95.

time-honored: respected or continued because of age or long-term existence or use. Page 54.

to-and-fro: characterized by alternate movement forward (to) and backward (*fro,* or from). Page 64.

top: the part of a plant growing above ground, as distinct from the root. Page 89.

Toronto Daily Star: the highest-circulation newspaper in Canada, the *Toronto Daily Star* (since 1971 called the *Toronto Star*) has been in operation since 1892. Toronto is the largest city in Canada, located in the southeastern part of the country, on Lake Ontario. Page 99.

touchstone: a standard by which something is judged. From the literal meaning of *touchstone,* a hard, black stone formerly used to test the purity of gold and silver according to the color of the streak left when the metal was rubbed against it. Page 115.

trace element(s): one of several types of chemical elements required in minute quantities for healthy growth and development of plants and animals. (An *element* is a basic unit of matter, a substance that cannot be broken down into a simpler one by a chemical reaction.) Also called *essential element* or *trace mineral.* Page 76.

transcendent: going beyond ordinary limits or range—for example, of thought or belief; surpassing or exceeding the usual. Page 3.

transfixed: made motionless with wonder, amazement, etc. Page 94.

transistorized: equipped with transistors. A *transistor* is a small electronic device that acts to vary the flow of current in an electric circuit. During the 1950s and 1960s, transistors replaced the larger devices, *vacuum tubes,* sealed glass tubes containing a near-vacuum that allow the free passage of electric current. Using transistors enabled electronic equipment to be made smaller than with vacuum tubes. Page 87.

trauma: emotional shock following a stressful event. Page 85.

travail: pain or suffering resulting from conditions that are mentally or physically difficult to overcome. Page 85.

trellised: using a structure of light wooden or metal bars, which provides support for growing plants. Page 22.

Tritox: an outdoor insecticide, used for controlling insects that are harmful to plants. Page 72.

truss(es): a cluster of flowers or fruit on a single branching stem—for example, on a tomato plant. Page 32.

tuber: a fleshy, swollen part of a root. Page 66.

tuberous-rooted begonia: a *begonia,* a widely grown houseplant and garden plant with ragged-edged leaves and brightly colored flowers, that is grown from a *tuber,* a fleshy, swollen part of a root. Tuberous-rooted begonias are one of the basic types of begonias, other types having roots that are not tuberous. Page 66.

tungsten: a reference to a bulb, or light from a bulb, that uses the element *tungsten,* a bright-gray metallic element. A typical tungsten bulb is the common light bulb, which has a filament made of tungsten. (A *filament* is a thin wire that, when an electric current passes through it, lights up inside an electric light bulb.) Page 20.

turf fibre: the surface of soil (turf) with the fibres (also *fibers,* long, thin parts of plants), such as stems, roots, etc., growing in it. Page 23.

turnip: a vegetable that is the white or yellow rounded root of the turnip plant. Turnips usually measure from 2 to 3 inches (5 to 8 centimeters) in diameter when harvested and weigh between ½ and 1 pound (225 and 450 grams). Page 25.

turns, by: one thing following after another. Page 113.

𝒰

ultraviolet: a wavelength that is shorter than violet in the color spectrum, making it invisible to the human eye. The *color spectrum* is a rainbowlike series of colors, in the order violet, blue, green, yellow, orange and red. Each color has a different wavelength, red being the longest, progressing through the colors to violet (at the opposite end), the shortest. Page 29.

up against it: facing difficulty or danger. Page 66.

upper one acre: an *acre* is a unit of land area equal to 4,840 square yards (0.405 hectare). Hence *upper one acre,* an acre situated at a higher level or farther north. Page 23.

𝒱

vegetal: relating to, involving or typical of vegetables or other plants. Page 94.

vehemence: the quality of being *vehement,* expressing something with conviction or intense feeling. Page 113.

verdant: green with growing plants; having an abundance of vegetation. Also used figuratively to mean characterized by the spread of abundant new growth, as of ideas and actions. Page 3.

veritable: being true or real; not false or imaginary. Page 3.

vine house: a greenhouse-like structure in which vines are tended and grown. Page 14.

vine(s): a plant having a long, slender stem that trails or creeps on the ground or climbs by winding itself about a support or holding onto a surface. Page 38.

vis-à-vis: in relation to. Page 115.

visionary: characterized by or given to ideas and plans that may not be workable in the present but that anticipate things that will or may come to be. Page 113.

void: totally lacking in (something). Page 66.

W

W: an abbreviation for *watt*. *See also* **watts.** Page 29.

wake of, in the: *wake* is the visible trail (of agitated and disturbed water) left by something, such as a ship, moving through water. Hence a condition left behind someone or something that has passed; following as a consequence. Page 1.

Warwickshire: a county in the central part of England. Until the mid-1970s, Warwickshire included the industrial city of Coventry, which was subsequently incorporated into the county of the West Midlands. Page 67.

Washington Star: a Washington, DC, daily newspaper that, during its 130-year history (1852–1981) was one of the major publications in the city. Page 94.

watering can: a container for water, typically of metal or plastic and having a spout with a perforated nozzle, for watering or sprinkling plants and flowers. Page 13.

waterlily: a plant whose large, round, flat leaves and cup-shaped, fragrant petals float on the surface of lakes and pools. Page 22.

watts: units of electrical power. A *watt* is a measurement of the rate of flow of energy; that is, how much electrical energy is flowing per unit of time. Page 40.

wavelength: the distance from peak to peak in a wave. Page 24.

weeded: freed of unwanted plants. Page 12.

whim(s): figuratively, a sudden desire or change of mind, especially one that is unusual or unexplained. Page 22.

Whitsun: the time period in early June falling on and just after *Whitsunday,* the Christian religious festival held to commemorate the day that, according to the Bible, the Holy Spirit (God in the form of a spirit) came to the followers of Jesus. The name means *White Sunday,* in reference to the white robes traditionally worn on that day by those newly baptized. Page 68.

wholesaler(s): one in the business of buying or selling goods in large amounts at low prices to shops and businesses, rather than the selling of goods in shops to customers. Page 91.

willow: a type of tree that has flexible branches and long, narrow, drooping leaves. Page 26.

wilt: 1. cause plants or leaves to droop or shrivel. Page 73.

   2. the drooping of plants or shriveling of leaves because of a lack of water, too much heat or disease. Page 107.

windbreak: a growth of trees, a structure of boards or the like, serving as a shelter from the wind. Page 77.

wither: (of a plant) become dry and shriveled; wrinkle and contract, or cause to wrinkle and contract, through loss of moisture. Page 13.

woe: cause of sorrow; trouble. Page 60.

Wonder, Stevie: (1950–) a highly praised American composer, singer and musician who recorded his first hit song in 1963, at the age of thirteen. He often uses his music as a force for social progress. Page 113.

worldview: a comprehensive conception or image of the universe and of humanity's relation to it; a conception of the course of events in and of the purpose of the world as a whole, forming a philosophical outlook on the universe. Page 115.

X

X-ray(s): invisible waves consisting of tiny particles of energy that are able to go through soft materials in the same way that light passes through glass. They are called *X-rays* because, at the time of their discovery, they were rays of an unknown origin. They are commonly used by hospitals and doctors to show pictures of the inside of the body. Page 10.

Y

yield: the quantity or amount given forth or produced as a result of efforts taken to improve the growth of plants or crops. Page 1.

Z

Zurich, University of: an institution of higher learning located in Zurich, Switzerland. Founded in 1833, it is the largest university in Switzerland and one of the leading research universities in Europe. Page 113.

INDEX

A

"agrotechnical" methods, 12

air temperature

control of, 49

ammonium sulphate

potash and, 42

aphis

ladybirds (ladybugs) and, 73

paraffin emulsion and, 73

atomic and molecular theory

George Washington University, 9

atomic gardening, 103

Atomic Gardening Society, 10, 103

atomic seeds, 103–104

auditing

definition, 85

Australia

plant experiments, 113

automatic controls

greenhouse, 47

B

Backster, Cleve

CIA, plant experiments, 113

ball-cock

control of water and, 47

photograph, 51

barnyard fertilizers

avoiding, 90

BBC interviews

L. Ron Hubbard on horticultural
discoveries, 1, 87

bedding plants

humidity, 17

peat moss pots and watering of, 17

temperature, 16

watering, 16

begonias

    answers to troubles with, 67

    brown spots, 77

    infra-red and, 67

    troubles with, 66

black spot

    lack of sun and, 76

blight, 91

    plants and, 101

bowl fires, 48

British *Farmers Weekly*

    L. Ron Hubbard plant discoveries
        and, 115

British television

    L. Ron Hubbard and experimental plant
        laboratory, 1, 87

brown spots

    tests, 76–77

bugs

    handling, 93

C
_____

Can plants think?, 93, 97

carrots, 93

    peat moss and, 55

    sand as humus, 65

Cartwright, J.

    letter to LRH, 74–75

Cedar of Lebanon

    photograph, 78

    Ron sweeping snow from, 78

change

    recovery and, 107–109

    root of departures and, 107

chemicals

    use of clean chemicals, 90

China

    cyclical famine and lack of agricultural
        know-how, 9

chrysanths

    answers to troubles with, 73, 76

    chrysanthemum leaf miner, 73

    insecticides and, 72

    ladybirds (ladybugs) and, 73

    soft radiation and, 76

    spray being used on, 77

    troubles with, 72, 74

CIA

    plant research and, 113

cistern

    heating water and feeding plants, 47

    switch, 49

cloche growing, 76

cold frames

    temperature, 17

    watering, 17

commercial growers

    continuous outflow without much
        inflow, 91

    disease and snipping tops, 89

    failures and revenge taken out on
        plants, 91

    opinions, attitudes and practices of, 91

reactive attitude toward plants, 91

"stuck flow" and, 91

communication

plants and, 87

compost

leaf mould, 55

peat moss, 55

sowing seeds and, 61

corn

Golden Bantam Hybrid, 23

South American Popcorn, 26

see also **sweet corn**

crops

home food supply, 63

size and yield, 1

speeding growth of, 91

cucumbers, 93

growing, 17, 33–34, 47

photograph of plants, 48

temperature, 17

tungsten lights

left on all night, 47

switched off part of the night, 47

tungsten light test, 52

watering, 17

cuttings, 18

𝒟
_____

Data Series

Dianetics and Scientology and, 106

day and night

light, 93

DDT

bugs and, 93

definitions

auditing, 85

E-Meter, 85

Dianetics, 88

Data Series and, 106

L. Ron Hubbard, Founder, 7

disease

amputate out of a greenhouse, 21

avoiding disease-killers injurious to the plants, 90

causes, 76

choosing disease-resistant strains, 89

control, 9

disease-free food, 20

dying and, 101

freedom from, 89

handling, 76

human and plant, 103

mental/spiritual trauma and, 88

moisturization constant, less disease, 70

plants and "state of mind," 100, 101

shock and, 89, 91

willingness of plants to grow and, 89

winter and, 38

dynamics

description, 102

plants and, 102

E

East Grinstead

Saint Hill Manor, 1

East Grinstead Courier, 7, 62

articles, 63, 93

horticultural experimentation, 7

economics

handling stuck flow of the workers, 91

worry over and growing plants, 91

electrodes, 85, 93

Electropsychometer (E-Meter)

definition, 85

electrodes and, 93

photograph, 87

plants and, 97

tomato plants and, 86, 93, 96, 100

environmental consciousness, 3

ES lampholders, 40

ever-bearing, 38

experimental ledger book

L. Ron Hubbard's handwritten notations, 30–31

experimental procedure, 22

Experimental Project 1, 23

Experimental Project 3, 25–29

original project notes, 24

F

fallout

series of lectures addressing, 9

Farmers Weekly, **British**

L. Ron Hubbard plant discoveries and, 115

Farmers' Weekly, **South Africa**

article on LRH and plant experiments, 100–101

feeding

plants and, 18–20

watering/heating/feeding system, 51

fertilizer, 9

application of, 20

barnyard, avoiding, 90

cutting down on, 21

watering and, 20

Fifth Dynamic, 102

life and, 102

plants and, 103

flavor

minerals and, 20

plant feeding and, 18

flowers, 18

automated greenhouse for cultivation of, 3

begonias, *see* **begonias**

chrysanths, *see* **chrysanths**

geraniums, *see* **geraniums**

greenhouse designs for flower cultivation in American Northwest winters, 7

growing in a greenhouse, 18

heat and humidity and faster growth of, 18

orchid, *see* **orchid**

pinks, 76

roses

    ladybirds (ladybugs) and, 73

food

    disease-free, 20

    experimental goal of food production, 7

    increasing the world's food supply, 97, 103

    revitalizing the world's food resources, 86

    supply of, 63

"food of the gods," 3

free-form English gardening, 12

fruiting

    picking and, 90

    when to pick, 90

fungus

    bottom heat and, 38

    infra-red light and control of, 40

G

galvanometer, 100

gamma rays, 33

gardeners

    green thumb, 21

Garden News

    articles on LRH plant experiments, 33–35, 37–43, 44, 47–53, 55–59, 65, 79–80

    introduction, 32

    L. Ron Hubbard asked readers to join in his experiments, 65

George Washington University

    original US class on atomic and molecular theory, 9

geraniums

    infra-red light and, 44

    light and growth and, 37, 44

    light test, photograph, 44

    mercury vapour light and, 37

    Saint Hill Manor, 10

    tungsten light and, 44

germination, 23, 60

    high rate of, 61

    new sowing technique, 61

    temperature and, 16

glasshouse, *see* **greenhouse**

Golden Bantam Hybrid corn, 23

Golden Hummer corn, 23, 26

gravel planting bed

    photograph, 16

greenhouse

    automated, 3, 46–53

    automatic controls, 47

    dangers of, 14

    dries out accidentally, handling, 90

    earth black with water, 14

    hiring personnel for, 21

    humidity, 13–14, 18

    laboratory at Saint Hill Manor, 1

    mildew, how to handle, 38–43

    plant feeding, 18

    purpose, 14

    temperature, 16, 18, 49

thermostat, 47, 49

watering, 13–14

green light

soil and, 38

green thumb

description, 21

Grounds Manager, 52

duties of, 12–21

Herbert D. Hall, 12

grower, *see* **commercial growers**

grow lights, 3, 24, 36

H

Hall, Herbert D.

Grounds Manager, Saint Hill, 12, 52

inspecting orchid, photograph, 2

photograph of L. Ron Hubbard and, 12

Hall, O. T.

letter to LRH, 66

heating, 47

ratio of humidity, light and heat, 89

watering/heating/feeding system, 51

Helena, Montana

LRH's boyhood home, 7

hiring

personnel to work with plants, 21, 90

horticulture

discoveries of considerable interest
to, 117

early interest in, 7

LRH revolutionized the world of, 3

research in, 103

hose

watering and, 13

Hudson, N. W.

letter from L. Ron Hubbard to, 70

humidity

bedding plants, 16

change in, 107

cucumbers, 17

greenhouse, 13, 14, 18

plants do best in, 18

ratio of humidity and heat to
light, 89

sweet corn, 70

temperature and faster growth, 18

humus

fresh manure, 65

sand, 65

I

Ideal Scene, 109

infra-red, 33, 48

begonias and, 67

geraniums and, 44

growing seeds under, 93

growing tomatoes all year round, 101

heaters, 49

heating elements, 48

light bulbs, 40

mildew control and, 10, 38, 39

soil and warming it, 40

insect spray, 77

    test, 76

irrigation, 9

J

Jenks, O. C.

    letter to LRH, 68

jungle

    hot and humid, 18

L

ladybirds (ladybugs)

    aphides and, 73

law, natural

    change and, 106

"lazybones" method, 61

leaf mould

    plant growth and, 58

    quality compost, 55

    sowing techniques and, 61

letters to and from L. Ron Hubbard, 66–77

lettuce

    sand as humus, 65

life

    compartmentalization of life into eight
        dynamic urges, 102

    presence of, in plants, 100

life energies, 1

life forms

    plants and other, 103

life sources, 1, 103

light

    artificial plant light, 36

    colors, 37, 38

    day and night, 93

    experimentation, 36

    geraniums and, 44

    green, soil and, 38

    grow lights, 3, 24, 36

    infra-red, *see* infra-red

    mercury vapour, *see* mercury vapour
        light

    on all night and mildew control, 47

    outdoor, 44

    plants and, 36

    purple, geraniums and, 37

    ratio of heat and humidity and, 89

    shaded greenhouse, 44

    sodium type, 37

    street light and plants, 37

    test, 43

    tungsten, *see* tungsten light

    ultra-violet, *see* ultra-violet light

light spectrum analysis

    growth rate and, 10

logic

    codification of, 106

"look, don't think," 33

M

Maharajah of Jaipur

  Saint Hill Manor, East Grinstead, Sussex, 7

manure

  fresh, plant growth and, 65

material universe

  spiritual life energy and, 85

melons

  flavor, 18

  growing, 17–18

mental trauma

  disease and, 88

mercury vapour light

  geraniums, plant growth and, 37, 44

mildew

  cure for, 38–43

  infra-red light and control of, 39–40

  lack of sun and, 76

  lights and controlling, 47

  sprays, 76, 77

minerals

  application of, 20

  flavor and, 20

  plants and, 76, 77

  soil and, 20, 77

  use of, 90

min–max thermometer, 49

moisturization, *see* **watering**

Montana

  LRH's boyhood home, 7

Moscow Agricultural Academy

  plant experiments, 113

mulch

  watering and, 17

mutation, 3, 9, 69, 76, 103

N

natural law

  change and, 106

Naval School of Military Government, Princeton University

  Taiwan and reformation of agricultural methods, 9

New Zealand's *Evening Post*

  L. Ron Hubbard and, 113

nitrates

  commercial, time to be effective, 20

O

orchid

  L. Ron Hubbard and H. D. Hall inspecting, photograph, 2

  treating, 40

P

pain

  plants and, 100

paraffin emulsion

  aphides and, 73

peaches

Saint Hill Manor, 10

peas, 93

sand as humus, 65

peat *moss*

carrots and, 55

failure, 55

pressed pots and watering, 17

personnel

green thumb and, 21

phosphates

commercial, time to be effective, 20

pinks, 76

plant feeding, 18–20

flavor and, 18

heating water and feeding plants, 47

plant kingdom

spiritual life energy and, 85

plants

blight and, 101

Can plants think?, 93, 97

change and recovery and, 107–109

commercial growers and reactive
attitude, 91

commercial surgery practices
omitted, 89

communication with, 87

disease

causes of, 76

freedom from, 89

handling, 76

thinking of dying, 101

E-Meter and

demonstration, 100

reactions and growth of
plants, 100

enthusiasm and, 21

feeding, *see* **plant feeding**

feelings and, 1, 113

Fifth Dynamic, 103

flavor and, 18

fresh manure and, 65

green thumb and, 21

growing day and night, 34

growing things that aren't susceptible
to injury, 90

humidity and, 18

infra-red and, *see* **infra-red**

inner life, 88

life forms and, 103

minerals and, 76, 77

pain and, 100

pain, worry and anxiety and, 115

personnel who damage, 90

presence of life, 100

reading the state of mind of, 97

research

summary of advanced
experimentation, 89

why done, 103

Scientology and, 103

shock of a traumatic nature, 89

soil, *see* **soil**

speeding growth, 91

spiritual life energy and, 85

spraying, 20

suppression of the impulse to survive
and, 89

tests on vegetables, vines, corn, root
crops, 56

tomato, *see* **tomato plants**

transplanting of, 90

traumatic shock and, 89

watering, *see* **watering**

willingness to grow, 89

worry and, 100

pole-beans, 93

potash

ammonium sulphate and, 42

potato sprays, 76

potting house

watering, 14

Princeton University

papers on Taiwan's agricultural
methods, 9

product

outflow of product without much
inflow, 91

purple light

geraniums and, 37

R

radiation

seeds and, 33, 38

soft, *see* **soft radiation**

sweet corn and, 39

tomato plants growing
and, 38, 42

radioactive fallout

series of lectures addressing, 9

radishes, 93

reactive attitude

commercial growers and plants, 91

recovery, 107–109

research

LRH asks readers to join in his
experiments, 65

Rhodesia

letter from L. Ron Hubbard to
Mr. Hudson in, 70

root crops

tests on, 56

roots

improper watering of, 13

transplanting a tree and, 80

warm water at, 47

root systems

protection of, 90

roses

ladybirds (ladybugs) and, 73

rotated crops

agricultural method of, 9

S

Saint Hill Manor, 7

greenhouse laboratory, 1

path to glasshouse, photograph, 8

photograph, 4–5

photograph of L. Ron Hubbard in his
office, 11

photographs of L. Ron Hubbard, viii, 6

Saint Hill Manor Horticultural Research Centre, 46, 54, 61, 103

    ledger book of handwritten notations on research, 31

    photographs, 8, 9

    see also **Sussex Research Station**

salad symphony, 99

sand

    humus for certain plants, 65

Scientology, 88

    applied religious philosophy, 3

    auditing, 85

    Data Series and, 106

    living things and, 91

    L. Ron Hubbard, Founder, 7

    plants and, 103

Secret Life of Plants, The

    Stevie Wonder and, 113, 115

seed boxes

    assisting germination in, 16

    watering, 14

seeds

    irradiation of, 32

    mutation, 3

    radiation and, 38, 42

    X-rays and, 101, 103

SHE Magazine

    article on LRH and plant experiments, 97

shock

    commercial growers and snipping tops, 89

    minimum shock to plants, 90

    plants, death and, 89

    plants, disease and poor quality and, 91

    result of shocking plants into production, 91

    traumatic, plants and, 89

Shuff, Derek H., 102

    administrative aide and publicity manager, 60

sodium-type light, 37

soft radiation, 3, 9, 32

    chrysanths and, 76

soil

    green light and, 38

    heated, 52

    infra-red and warming, 40

    minerals and, 20, 77

    pot test for the perfect, 56, 59

    sterilizing, 73, 90

    test for the perfect growing soil, 56–59, 61

    test of adequate watering, 14

    trace elements and, 76, 77

    transplanting a tree, 79

    watering, 51

    watering a cold frame, 17

soil management, 9

South Africa

    Farmers' Weekly, article on LRH and plant experiments, 100

    The Natal Witness, article, 114

sowing technique

    new, 61

    soil and, 54

soya beans

    nutritionally rich, 9

spirit

    isolation of, 3

    vegetable life and, 3

spiritual life energy

    material universe and, 85

    plant kingdom and, 85

spiritual trauma

    disease and, 88

spraying

    avoiding heavy sprays, 90

    healthy plants and, 20

    sprinklers and, 21

    tests, 76

    when done, 21

sprinkler (system)

    photograph, 15

    spraying and, 21

    use of, 13, 14

"state of mind"

    plants and disease, 100

street light

    plants and, 37

string beans

    flavor, 18

    growing, 18

strip lighting, 40

stuck flow

    growers and, 91

    handling, 91

survival

    heavy suppression of the impulse to
       survive and, 89

Sussex

    Saint Hill Manor, 1

Sussex Research Station, 22, 24, 55

    photographs, 8, 9

    see also **Saint Hill Manor Horticultural
       Research Centre**

sweet corn, 93

    changes and, 108–109

    first sweet corn crop raised, 62, 63

    Golden Hummer corn, 23, 26

    moisturization, 70

    radiation and, 39

    sand as humus, 65

    tests on, 56

    watering, 70

sweet peas

    type of light and, 37

T
_____

Taiwan

    reformation of agricultural
       methods, 9

temperature

    bedding plants, 16

    change in, 107

control of, 49

cucumbers, 17

flowers, 18

germination and, 16

greenhouse, 14, 16, 18, 49

humidity and, 13

   faster growth, 18

melons, 17

ratio of temperature to light and
   humidity, 89

regulation, 9

tomato plants, 16

vegetables, 18

vine crops, 18

watering and, 50

thermometer

min–max, 49

registering the soil
   temperature, 52

thermostats

greenhouse, 47, 49

photograph, 15

This Week **magazine,** 98

time switches, 47

tobacco, 93

tomato plants, 93

answers to troubles with, 76

changes and, 108

coloured lights and, 38, 43

E-Meter

   demonstration, 100

experiments, 93

photographs, 86, 96

growing, 33, 42

infra-red and growing all year
   round, 101

light test, photograph, 43

new strain, artificially mutated, 76

radiation and, 42

temperature, 16

troubles with, 74–75

X-rays and, 101

Toronto Daily Star, 99

trace elements

soil and, 76, 77

transplanting

avoiding, 90

methods of, 78–80

trees, 79–80

trees

transplanting, 79–80

tungsten light

clear, not pearl, 43

cucumber plant test, 52

geraniums and, 44

photographs of plants growing
   under, 20, 48

plant growth and, 44

results when left on all night, 47

results when switched off part of the
   night, 47

time clock for, 49

U

ultra-violet light, 29, 33

    geraniums and, 44

V

vegetable life

    same order of life as exists in Man, 3

vegetables

    heat and humidity and faster growth of, 18

    string beans, growing, 18

    tests on, 56

    watering and temperature, 18

ventilation

    change in, 107

vine crops

    heat and humidity and faster growth of, 18

    tests on, 56

    watering and temperature, 18

vine house

    watering, 14

W

watering, 47

    bedding plants, 16

    change in, 107

    cold frames, 17

    constant of, 70

    cucumbers, 17

    dry weather and, 13

    experiment results, 41

    fertilizing and, 20

    flowers, 18

    greenhouse, 13, 14

    heating water and feeding plants, 47

    hose and, 13

    light and heat and, 89

    melons, 17

    mulch and, 17

      melons and, 17

    peat-moss pots with bedding plants, 17

    potting house, 14

    routine, 13

    seed boxes, 14

    sprayer, 13

    sprinkler, 13

    temperature and, 18, 50, 52

    vegetables, 18

    vine crops, 18

    warm water at roots, 47

    watering can, 13

    watering/heating/feeding system, 51

watering can

    use of, 13, 14

wholesalers

    produce brought back from, 91

Why

what changed, 107

windbreak, 77

Wonder, Stevie

The Secret Life of Plants and, 113, 115

worms

heat and, 20

worry

plants and, 100

$\mathcal{X}$

X-rays, 33

plant growth and, 101

seeds and, 69, 103

$\mathcal{Z}$

Zurich, University of

plant experiments, 113

THE
L. RON HUBBARD
SERIES

"To really know life," L. Ron Hubbard wrote, "you've got to be part of life. You must get down and look, you must get into the nooks and crannies of existence. You have to rub elbows with all kinds and types of men before you can finally establish what he is."

Through his long and extraordinary journey to the founding of Dianetics and Scientology, Ron did just that. From his adventurous youth in a rough and tumble American West to his far-flung trek across a still mysterious Asia; from his two-decade search for the very essence of life to the triumph of Dianetics and Scientology—such are the stories recounted in the L. Ron Hubbard Biographical Publications.

Drawn from his own archival collection, this is Ron's life as he himself saw it. With each volume of the series focusing upon a separate field of endeavor, here are the compelling facts, figures, anecdotes and photographs from a life like no other.

Indeed, here is the life of a man who lived at least twenty lives in the space of one.

FOR FURTHER INFORMATION VISIT
www.lronhubbard.org

To order copies of *The L. Ron Hubbard Series*
or L. Ron Hubbard's Dianetics and
Scientology books and lectures, contact:

US AND INTERNATIONAL

BRIDGE PUBLICATIONS, INC.
5600 E. Olympic Blvd.
Commerce, California 90022 USA
www.bridgepub.com
Tel: (323) 888-6200
Toll-free: 1-800-722-1733

UNITED KINGDOM AND EUROPE

NEW ERA PUBLICATIONS
INTERNATIONAL ApS
Smedeland 20
2600 Glostrup, Denmark
www.newerapublications.com
Tel: (45) 33 73 66 66
Toll-free: 00-800-808-8-8008